To everyone
who enjoys fresh natural food
as much as we do

NEW COVENT GARDEN
SOUP COMPANY'S

Soup & Beyond

SOUPS, BEANS AND OTHER THINGS

MACMILLAN

ACKNOWLEDGMENTS
Executive Editor: Kate Kime
Editor: Julia Laflin
Consultant Editor: Caroline Jeremy
Designer: Claire Fry
Illustrator: Serena Feneziani
Recipes tested by: Jo Gilks, Gilly Booth, Paul Bloomfield, Antonia Locke, Clare Anderton, Sandra Jordan, Susannah Senior and many others.

New Covent Garden Soup Company would like to thank everyone who so generously gave us their recipes and are happy to share them with all who read this book. Too many to list in this space, they are mentioned on the recipes themselves.

We would also like to thank Gayle Hart and Alex Cox who so tirelessly checked the copy for mistakes.

While we have made every effort to trace any copyright holders of recipes, we welcome notification of any errors or omissions and will make best effort to correct these in future editions

First published 1999 by Macmillan
an imprint of Pan Macmillan Publishers Ltd
20 New Wharf Road, London N1 9RR
Basingstoke and Oxford
Associated companies throughout the world
www.panmacmillan.com

ISBN-10: 0-333-75226-0
ISBN-13: 978-0-333-75226-5

A CIP catalogue record for this book is available from the British Library

Printed and bound in Great Britain
by Butler & Tanner Ltd

Contents

Introduction

Ever since we published our first book we have been dreaming of writing a second. Every new recipe and every new idea has caused a flurry of excitement as the book took form in our minds. Even the other foods we explored during this time: gravies, sauces and beans, inspired more ideas and increased our enthusiasm. With a multinational team and friends generous enough to share their new discoveries, we have built up a collection of recipes inspired by cultures and countries the world over. Eventually the itch to put pen to paper was too much.

The three of us, Kate, Caroline and Julia, together with our many patient testers, spent hours in one another's kitchens trying out and tasting our way through over 200 different recipes to whittle them down to our absolute favourites.

Recipes appeared from everywhere – our Factory Manager's soup recipe procured from a Finnish train driver while he was en route from St Petersburg; our former Managing Director's favourite cassoulet he created to use up his mountain of home-grown dried broad beans; one of our development cook's traditional Mexican bean dishes that has been in her family for generations. We could go on and on.

Never before had we eaten so much and so well. Each recipe was tested up to 3 or 4 times to make sure it was foolproof. We had such fun, but got so fat!

Claire, our designer, really had her work cut out. She handwrote every single page, often through the night (at the last count she was on her 70th black pen)!

1

This time we decided to include all the non-soup recipes we have been wanting to share for years. The book is divided into 5 main sections: stocks, soups, beans, breads and other things.

The 'stocks' we have taken from our 'Book of Soups'. Fundamental to every good soup, they really make the difference between a fairly ordinary broth and something with an extraordinary depth of flavour. Just make a whole load and store them in your freezer until needed.

As we spend every day thinking about soup, 'soup' is the biggest chapter. The wonderful thing about making soup is that the possibilities are endless. You can use almost any ingredients - meat, fish, vegetables, fruit, grains, pulses, alcohol, spices - and get a fantastic result. All you need is good fresh ingredients and a good-quality stock.

Every few weeks our team of cooks dreams up a new recipe. A walk through a market, a holiday abroad, a meal in a restaurant or an afternoon in the garden can all spark off a new idea. The New Covent Garden Soup Company kitchen teems with activity as new ideas are put to the test. Here we have shared our favourite creations, together with some wonderful recipes so generously sent in to us.

One of our latest passions is beans. We feel they are vastly underrated and add a whole new dimension to food in terms of taste and texture. When cooked with meat they soak up the fat and juices and the result just melts in your mouth; with salads and salsas they give interest and texture without the bulk of rice and potatoes. They are also a natural ingredient in soups, casseroles and fritters. We have indulged ourselves slightly by including this chapter, but we hope you'll be inspired to pick up a pan and give a few of them a try.

Bread is a natural companion to soup, making it a meal in itself. Not all bread needs hours of kneading and proving and they really do taste so much better when freshly made. We explored all our favourites, including soda bread, yoghurt bread and scones. Once we'd started we realised we could have filled a whole book.

Finally the 'other things'. A swirl of cream, freshly chopped herbs and a handful of croûtons are ideal for some occasions, but it's such fun being a bit more creative and using other things to add texture, flavour, substance or colour. A dollop of mashed potato in a creamy fresh soup turns it into a filling meal; a sweet and tangy salsa on a hot and spicy soup brings the whole thing alive; flavoured dumplings plonked in a clear broth look really impressive. Try them. You'll find soup and beans take on a whole new dimension.

Someone once summed up the New Covent Garden Soup Company as 'a group of enthusiastic and creative cooks who make delicious and natural food for busy people.' That is our dream.

This book would not have been possible without the help of everyone at 'Soup', our friends and our families. We thank them all for their generosity, patience and support.

I hope you enjoy your journey through this book as much as we enjoyed writing it.

Enjoy your journey through this book

INDIAN
OCEAN

ATLANTIC
OCEAN

PACIFIC
OCEAN

Stocks

Stocks

Many people are either frightened of making stock or they can't be bothered, believing it to be time-consuming and not worth the effort. Unfortunately, much as we welcome anything that saves us time, a stock that is good, fresh and home-made really makes a difference to a recipe. Perhaps it is even more important in soup-making because the liquid makes up such a large proportion of the final dish.

Because of its fantastic depth of flavour, a good stock will turn a simple recipe into something really special. In particular, a home-made meat stock will add richness and body in a way a stock cube never can. It is also more nutritious, carrying with it so much goodness from the ingredients used.

Use leftover carcasses, buy off-cuts from your butcher or use the process as a way of poaching meat which can then be stripped off the bone and eaten. Make a big pot when you have time and then freeze what you don't need in half pint batches.

Stock-making really is terribly straight-forward. Just remember the following:

— The quality of the stock is dictated by its ingredients. Remember the combination of flavours will not only transfer to the stock, but also the final dish

— Give the stock plenty of time to develop when cooking - resist the temptation to stir and fiddle, although you should skim off the impurities now and then

— If you want a clear stock, bring the water to the boil from cold and simmer very gently. Strain carefully, letting the moisture drip through the sieve. Don't push the contents through or you will get bits that will make it cloudy. If necessary, strain again, this time through muslin

— Finally, don't overseason. You can always add salt and pepper to the final dish, but you can't take it away

Chicken Stock

PREPARATION TIME: 15 minutes
COOKING TIME: RICH STOCK: 3 hours
                   LIGHT STOCK: 1½ - 2 hours
MAKES: 2.25 litres (4 pints)

1.5 kg (3lb 2oz) fresh chicken
1 medium onion stuck with 3 cloves
2 medium carrots, coarsely sliced
2 medium sticks celery, coarsely sliced
unpeeled cloves of 1 head of garlic
6 sprigs of fresh flat-leaf parsley with stems
3 sprigs of fresh thyme
1 bay leaf
a pinch of salt
3 litres (5¼ pints) cold water to cover
                  by at least 7.5cm (3")

Place all the ingredients in a saucepan or stockpot. Cover and bring slowly to the boil. Reduce heat to a gentle simmer. Skim off any scum. Simmer very gently with the lid ajar for 2-3 hours for a rich stock and 1½-2 hours for a light stock, skimming from time to time. Do not disturb the stock or move it in any way. Strain well. Be careful not to force any of the ingredients through the sieve. Allow to cool. Refrigerate. Skim off any fat.

Lamb Stock

PREPARATION TIME : 40 minutes
COOKING TIME: 4 hours
MAKES : 1.2 litres (2 pints)

Pre-heat the oven to 240°C / 475°F / Gas Mark 8

900g (2lb) lamb bones, including meat trimmings
        but excluding any fat, chopped into
        small pieces by your butcher
½ small onion, roughly chopped
1 small carrot, roughly chopped
1 stick celery, roughly chopped
2 button mushrooms, roughly chopped
2.25 litres (4 pints) water
1 bay leaf
1 sprig of fresh mint
1 sprig of fresh thyme
1 garlic clove, bruised

Put the lamb bones into a roasting tin and roast in the
oven for about 45 minutes, or until the bones and trimmings
are well browned but are not burnt. Drain off and
reserve any fat and put the bones into a large saucepan.

Put 1 tablespoon of the reserved fat into a medium-
sized saucepan. Fry the onion, carrot, celery and
mushrooms over a moderate heat for about 15
minutes until well browned but not burnt, stirring
frequently. Add to the large saucepan of bones, together
with the water, bay leaf, sprigs of mint and thyme and
the garlic clove. Cover, bring to the boil and simmer
very gently, uncovered, for 3 hours, removing any
fat from the surface as it collects. Pass through a fine
sieve into a bowl. Cool, then chill in the refrigerator
overnight. Remove any fat from the surface and the
stock is then ready for use.

Beef Stock

PREPARATION TIME: 1 hour
COOKING TIME: 3½ hours
MAKES: 3 litres (5 pints)

3.7 Kg (8lb) beef bones (shin, leg or ribs)
6 litres (10½ pints) water to cover
1 tablespoon sunflower oil
2 small onions, halved and unskinned
2 medium carrots, coarsely sliced
2 medium leeks, coarsely sliced
a few fresh parsley stalks
2 small sprigs of fresh thyme
2 bay leaves
15 black peppercorns
a pinch of salt

If you would like a dark stock, pre-heat the oven to 200°C/
400°F/ Gas Mark 6 and roast the bones in a roasting tin
for about 30-40 minutes until well browned, and then
proceed with the recipe below.

Wash the bones well, then put them into a large saucepan
or stockpot with the water. Cover and bring slowly to the
boil. Reduce the heat to a gentle simmer. Skim off any
scum. Simmer very gently with the lid ajar for about
1½ hours, skimming from time to time.

Meanwhile, heat the oil and sauté the onions over a
moderate heat until well browned, but do not burn. Add
them to the bones and water, together with the
remaining ingredients. Bring back to the boil. Reduce
the heat to a gentle simmer. Skim off any scum. Simmer
very gently with the lid ajar for another 2 hours,
skimming from time to time. Do not disturb the stock
or move it in any way. Strain well. Be careful not to
force any of the ingredients through the sieve. Allow
to cool. Refrigerate. Skim off any fat.

If you would like a richer stock with more depth of
flavour, once the stock has been refrigerated and the
fat removed, put it into a clean saucepan and simmer
until it is reduced by evaporation to the required strength.

Game Stock

PREPARATION TIME: 40 minutes
COOKING TIME: 2 hours 30 minutes
MAKES: 2 litres (3½ pints)

1.5Kg (3lb 5oz) scraps and bones of the roasted, or fresh,
        carcasses of 2 pheasants or other game
3-4 medium onions, quartered
2 medium carrots, coarsely sliced
1 turnip, coarsely sliced (optional)
a small bunch of fresh parsley stalks
1 tablespoon whole allspice
2 teaspoons black peppercorns
1 bay leaf
a pinch of salt
3 litres (5 pints) of cold water to cover

Place all the ingredients in a large saucepan or
stockpot. Cover and bring to the boil. Reduce the heat
to a gentle simmer. Skim off the scum. Simmer
very gently with the lid ajar for 3 hours,
skimming from time to time. Do not disturb the
stock or move in any way. Strain well. Be careful
not to force any of the ingredients through the
sieve. Allow to cool. Refrigerate. Skim off any fat.

Fish Stock

1 Kg (2lb 2oz) fish bones, heads and trimmings
from non-oily fish, broken up
and rinsed under cold water
1 medium onion, roughly chopped
2 medium carrots, coarsely sliced
1 medium leek, coarsely sliced
1 medium stick celery, coarsely sliced
¼ head of Florence fennel, sliced
3 sprigs of fresh flat-leaf parsley with stems
3 sprigs of fresh thyme
1 bay leaf
a pinch of salt
2.5 litres (4¾ pints) cold water to cover

Place all the ingredients in a saucepan or stockpot. Cover
and bring slowly to the boil. Reduce heat to a gentle
simmer. Skim off any scum. Simmer very gently with
the lid ajar for 30 minutes, skimming from time to
time. Do not disturb the stock or move it in any way.
Strain well. Be careful not to force any of the
ingredients through the sieve. Allow to cool. Refrigerate.

Fish stock does not need as much simmering as other
stocks. Too much cooking will result in the bones
giving off a bitter flavour.

Vegetable Stock

PREPARATION TIME: 20 minutes
COOKING TIME: 1 hour 45 minutes
MAKES: 2.7 litres (4½ pints)

3 medium onions, roughly chopped
5 medium carrots, roughly chopped
3 medium leeks, coarsely sliced
3 medium sticks celery, roughly chopped
8 cabbage leaves, sliced
1 head of full flavoured green lettuce, sliced
6 sprigs of fresh flat-leaf parsley
　　　　with stems, roughly chopped
3 sprigs of fresh thyme
1 bay leaf
a pinch of salt
3.5 litres (6 pints) cold water to cover

Place all the ingredients in a saucepan or stockpot. Cover and bring slowly to the boil. Reduce heat to a gentle simmer. Skim off any scum. Simmer very gently with the lid ajar for 1 hour, skimming from time to time. Do not disturb the stock or move it in any way. Strain well. Be careful not to force any of the ingredients through the sieve, as this will cloud the stock. Allow to cool. Refrigerate.

Soups

Soups

Soup-making is a tradition that goes back for thousands of years. Originally just a basic sustenance, soup was a warming and nourishing meal that brought the family together around the hearth.

Popular the world-over, it even played an important role in the earliest restaurant. The first eaterie to be actually known as a 'restaurant' was opened by a Parisian soup vendor, M. Boulanger, in 1765. He only served soups. The motto inscribed in Latin above his door translated as 'Come to me all of you whose stomachs cry out and I will restore you'.

Popular throughout the world, soup is arguably the most versatile meal you can cook. It can be made from almost anything, in any combination, and can be as thick, thin, robust, elegant, sophisticated, simple or unusual as you like. Hot soups are as warming and sustaining in the middle of winter as cold soups are refreshing and cooling in the heat of summer. They are also easy to digest and wonderfully soothing. They conjure up warm recollections of childhood, family meals and holidays. To hear someone reminiscing about their favourite soup is like looking at a snapshot of their past.

There are many so-called rules to soup-making. We believe the following are the most important:

— Use the best quality ingredients you can – the fresher the better

— Wherever possible try to use vegetables and fruit in season, they will taste better and probably be cheaper

— Don't add too much salt or it will destroy rather than enhance the flavour. Season just before serving and the true flavour will be given a wonderfully fresh lift

— Do use cream or milk to add richness, but don't add too much – it will overpower the flavour

— Texture can make or break a soup. Use a blender or liquidiser to give a fluffy, velvet-like texture to blended soups. Sadly food processors and handheld blenders do not give quite the same effect

— Under cooking and overcooking can destroy both flavour and texture. Some flavours need time to develop, some meats require tenderising, but others just as easily go into decline if cooked too long

Potato, Leek & Lavender Soup

(V) (F)

When creating new soup recipes, we love to take a traditional classic and give it a new twist. Many herbs and flowers are used in cooking, but we felt one in particular, lavender, has been rather overlooked. A herb by definition, lavender has been used in food for hundreds of years. It is also well known for its powers of cleansing, healing and soothing. Apparently lion tamers regularly sprinkle lavender oil in cages to keep the animals docile! We added the flowers to a classic Vichyssoise to give it a wonderful floral aftertaste. Lavender is very potent, so be careful to stick to the quantity recommended; add too much and it'll taste as if you're eating one of your grandmother's lavender bags! As this soup is ideal garnished with edible flowers, also try substituting young rose petals or chive flowers for the lavender heads.

SERVES: 4
PREPARATION AND COOKING TIME: 50 minutes

50g (2oz) butter
450g (1lb) leeks, washed well and finely sliced
675g (1½lb) potatoes, peeled and roughly chopped
1.5 litres (2½ pints) vegetable stock (see page 14)
425ml (¾ pint) full cream milk
flowers of 3 lavender heads
2 tablespoons crème fraîche
salt

TO GARNISH:
12 lavender flowers on their stalks, 5cm (2") long

Melt the butter and cook the leeks gently for 5 minutes in a covered saucepan, without colouring. Add the potatoes, stock, milk and lavender flowers. Cover, bring to the boil and simmer gently for about 20-25 minutes until the vegetables are tender. Cool a little, then purée in a liquidiser until very smooth.

Return to a clean saucepan, stir in the crème fraîche and taste for seasoning. Thin the soup a little with water if required. Serve chilled and garnished with lavender flower heads.

Cold Watercress & Apple Soup

When Julian Bernstein sent us his recipe for this delicious and delicate dream of a soup, we had no idea that it had already won gold twice in the Jersey championships of the prestigious Salon Culinaire awards, an achievement that requires an incredible 90 international points. A restauranteur and hotelier, Julian owns the Sea Crest Hotel and Restaurant in Petit Port, St Brelade, and was originally given the recipe by his mother, Ruby.

Make sure you put a generous pile of apple in each bowl. The crunchiness is a perfect contrast to the smooth mousse-like soup.

SERVES: 4
PREPARATION AND COOKING TIME: 40 minutes

25g (1oz) butter
2 Spanish onions, finely chopped
1 tablespoon medium curry powder
2 bunches watercress
1 tablespoon cornflour
570ml (1 pint) chicken stock (see page 9)
290 ml (½ pint) milk
2 egg yolks
150ml (¼ pint) hot double cream
1 eating apple, peeled, cored and sliced
salt and freshly ground black pepper

TO GARNISH:
2 eating apples, peeled, cored and finely diced
juice of 1 lemon
4 sprigs watercress

Melt the butter and cook the onion gently until soft in a covered saucepan, without colouring. Stir in the curry powder and cook for 2 minutes, stirring. Add the watercress, reserving 1 large handful. Mix the cornflour with a little stock until smooth and add to the soup with the remaining stock. Bring to the boil and simmer gently for 10 minutes. Add the reserved watercress leaves and cook for a further 2 minutes. Whisk the egg yolks into the hot cream, then stir into the soup. Remove immediately from the heat, cool a little, then purée with the milk and apple in a liquidiser until completely smooth and mousse-like. Season to taste and chill well.

Mix the apple dice with the lemon juice to retain colour and serve the soup liberally garnished with the diced apple and sprigs of watercress. This soup is also delicious hot.

Parsnip, Rhubarb & Ginger Soup

Over 2000 people entered our 1998 'Create a Soup' competition in the Daily Telegraph. This creation of retired tropical agriculturalist Robert Austin, from South Petherton in Somerset, was the winner. Thane Prince, the Telegraph's WEEKEND COOK, helped us to choose the winning recipe. She declared at the final, 'Rhubarb and ginger is a classic combination in cooking, but blending this with parsnips to make a savoury soup is ingenious. The rhubarb really cuts through the sweetness of the parsnips and the result is both unusual and delicious'.

Robert was taught to cook by his mother while he was recuperating from a badly broken ankle in 1953. Cooking has become his hobby ever since, and he likes to use fresh, good quality, local ingredients.

SERVES: 4
PREPARATION AND COOKING TIME: 30 minutes
50g (2oz) butter
450g (1lb) parsnips, peeled and roughly chopped
225g (8oz) rhubarb, washed and roughly sliced
1 medium onion, finely sliced
2 teaspoons fresh root ginger, grated
1 tablespoon plain flour
850ml (1½ pints) chicken stock (see page 9)
2 teaspoons light brown muscovado sugar
salt and freshly ground black pepper

TO GARNISH:
2 tablespoons fresh flat leaf parsley, chopped

Melt the butter and cook the parsnips, rhubarb, onion and grated ginger for 5 minutes in a covered saucepan, without colouring. Add the flour and stir well. Add the stock and sugar and taste for seasoning. Bring to the boil, stirring constantly. Lower the heat and simmer gently for about 15 minutes until the vegetables are tender. Cool a little, then purée in a liquidiser until very smooth. Adjust the seasoning, then reheat gently and serve garnished with chopped fresh parsley.

Cucumber, Pea & Mint Soup

(V) (F)

A good pea and mint soup has been at the top of our 'wish list' for ages, but whenever we tried it, the result was always too sweet. When Gayle Hart joined the recipe development team she was given the job of trying again. She ignored all our previous attempts and started from scratch with great determination. It paid off, and the soup became one of our bestselling summer soups. It is best served ice-cold but can be served warm.

SERVES: 4
PREPARATION AND COOKING TIME: 45 minutes

2 tablespoons extra virgin olive oil
2 medium onions, finely chopped
1 garlic clove, crushed
175g (6oz) potato, peeled and roughly chopped
400g (14oz) frozen peas
450g (1lb) cucumber, peeled and roughly chopped
425ml (¾ pint) vegetable stock (see page 14)
1 tablespoon lemon juice
Salt and freshly ground black pepper
1 tablespoon fresh mint, chopped
50ml (2floz) milk
200ml (7floz) single cream

TO GARNISH:
1 tablespoon fresh mint, chopped

Heat the oil and cook the onions and garlic gently for 10 minutes in a covered saucepan, without colouring. Add the potato, peas and cucumber, cover and cook gently for 2 minutes. Add the stock and lemon juice. Taste for seasoning. Cover, bring to the boil and simmer gently for about 10 minutes until the vegetables are tender. Cool a little, then purée in a liquidiser until very smooth, then pass through a fine sieve. Stir in the mint, milk and cream and gently reheat without boiling. Serve garnished with chopped mint.

20

Wensleydale Cheese Soup

When Norman Chadwick, who works for Printpak Europe, one of our packaging suppliers, first told us about this soup he warned us that one helping would never be enough. He was right! The combination of Wensleydale and bacon with a good chicken stock and a dash of paprika elevates this soup to the addictive scale. Be warned though, it's quite rich so be careful with 2nd helpings! Norman is the 1st to admit that he is no expert at soup-making but he 'knows a good one when he tastes it'. This recipe was passed to him by the owners of The Black Swan pub in Middleham, Yorkshire, before they retired to Spain. Middleham has a medieval castle, and the pub was famous for being a haunt of Richard III's as well as for its splendid cheese soup.

SERVES: 4-6
PREPARATION AND COOKING TIME: 35 minutes

25g (1oz) butter
110g (4oz) smoked bacon, chopped finely
2 medium onions, finely diced
2 large carrots, finely chopped
1 clove garlic, finely chopped
1.5 litres (2½ pints) chicken stock (see page 9)
1 teaspoon paprika
250g (9oz) Wensleydale cheese, grated
freshly ground black pepper

Melt the butter in a medium sized saucepan and sauté the bacon, onion and carrot together over a medium heat for 3-5 minutes. Add the garlic and cook for a further 2-3 minutes. Add the chicken stock and paprika, cover, bring to the boil, then simmer for 20 minutes.

Cool before processing in a liquidiser until smooth, transfer back to the saucepan and reheat slowly, adding the grated cheese and, stirring well, season with black pepper to taste. Don't add salt, unless you are sure it needs it. Serve immediately.

Lentil & Bacon Soup

Crisis, the national charity for single homeless people, provides aid at all stages of homelessness, from emergency help on the street to deposit guarantee schemes enabling homeless people to find long-term homes in the private rented sector. We have supported Crisis for many years in numerous ways. Each week they take our surplus food to distribute at their shelters. One winter we launched this Lentil & Bacon Soup to raise awareness of the dozens of homeless people who needlessly die from the cold each year. Enough money was raised to provide 10,000 meals. Spare a thought as you eat this soup. Crisis do a fantastic job. Its donation hotline number is 0800 0384838. No one deserves to be left out in the cold.

SERVES: 4
PREPARATION AND COOKING TIME: 40 minutes
25g (1oz) butter
1 garlic clove, finely chopped
1 medium onion, peeled and thinly diced
175g (6oz) red lentils, rinsed well
50g (2oz) split peas, rinsed well
2 tablespoons tomato purée
1.5 litres (2½ pints) ham stock (see below)
110g (4oz) streaky bacon, finely chopped
175g (6oz) carrots, peeled and finely diced
1 tablespoon parsley, finely chopped

FOR THE STOCK: This is the ideal way to use the stock from cooking a 3.2kg (7lb) gammon joint with 2 tablespoons brown sugar, 2 tablespoons malt vinegar, 1 bay leaf and water to cover.

Melt the butter in a saucepan, then add the garlic and onion and sauté for 2-3 minutes, without colouring. Add the lentils, split peas and tomato purée, then cook for 2-3 minutes more stirring constantly to prevent sticking. Pour in the ham stock, bring to the boil, then turn down the heat and simmer for 20-25 minutes, until the lentils and split peas are soft. Process in a liquidiser until smooth, then return to the pan and add the bacon, carrot and parsley. Simmer for 12-15 more minutes until the carrot is tender and serve.

Prince & Pedlar Soup

When George Hudd read about one of our soup-creating competitions, he wanted to invent something really unusual. He cooked up some medlars from his neighbour's garden with some quince that he'd brought back from Turkey. He then had a bit of fun with their names. Native to Asia and Europe, medlars, a yellowish brown pear-shaped fruit, can be found growing wild in England. They are, in fact, related to the rose family. If picking them yourself, take care as medlars are only edible when they are overripe. Quince is related to the pear and originates from Southern Europe and Asia. When ripe the fruit is covered in fine down and, when picked, should be stored calyx downwards until softened. George, a former Secretary of the Bankers Club, is now retired. Not only does he love cooking, but he also finds time to add to his admirable collection of 104 scrapbooks of cuttings about interesting people, archaeology, history and cookery.

TIP: Medlars are hard to come by and have a short season. A russet apple makes a very good substitute as the skin and fruit is very similar in taste.

SERVES: 6
PREPARATION AND COOKING TIME: 40 minutes

50g (2oz) butter
575g (1lb 5oz) quince, (approx 3)
      peeled, cored and roughly chopped
1 medlar, peeled, cored and roughly chopped
1 teaspoon turmeric
1.25 litres (2¼ pints) chicken stock (see page 9)
3 tablespoons single cream
2 egg yolks
salt and freshly ground black pepper

Melt the butter in a saucepan and add the quince, medlar and turmeric. Cook over a low heat for 10 minutes. Add the stock, bring to the boil and then turn down the heat and simmer for 20 minutes. Take off the heat and leave to cool.

Process in a liquidiser until smooth, then return to the pan. Beat the cream and egg yolks together, add a ladle full of soup to this mixture then pour into the soup. Cook gently over a low heat until the mixture thickens, stirring continuously. Season to taste.

23

Parsnip & Orange Soup

After a life on the move with the Royal Navy, Tricia and Sam Fry, the parents of our indispensable designer Claire Fry, are now enjoying the fruits of their labours in their Dorset garden. In fact, having moved 23 times during her husband's career, Tricia is thinking about writing a guide book on creating instant gardens!

Their parsnips frequently win prizes at their local flower show in Whitchurch Canonicorum, whilst the rest of the crop is puréed and frozen to be turned into this very simple and down-to-earth soup. During Lent, when parishioners from each church in the Marshwood Vale take it in turns to hold a Lenten bread and soup lunch, Tricia always finds this is very popular.

SERVES : 4
PREPARATION AND COOKING TIME: 40 minutes

1.2 litres (2 pints) chicken stock (see page 9)
8 medium parsnips, peeled and roughly chopped
juice of 4 oranges
salt and freshly ground black pepper

TO GARNISH:
finely pared skin of 1 orange, cut into fine shreds or julienne
flesh of 1 orange divided into skinned segments

Bring the stock to the boil in a saucepan. Add the parsnips, cover and simmer gently until tender.

Put the orange julienne for the garnish in a small bowl and pour over boiling water. Leave for 1 minute, then drain and refresh under cold water.

Purée parsnips in a liquidiser until very smooth. Return to a clean saucepan, thin with a little water if necessary, add the orange juice and taste for seasoning. Reheat gently.

Serve the soup hot, garnished with orange segments and julienne and a sprinkling of freshly ground black pepper.

Lovage & Almond Soup

(V)

We have experimented using lovage in soup for a long time, but usually find the taste is too strong—the only success we had had was with our Lettuce and Lovage Soup. So we were delighted when Lee Steele sent us her lovage and almond recipe as it works like a dream. The rich flavour of the lovage, an aromatic herb which grows between April and September, forms the basis of this creamy soup, and is balanced by the crunchiness of the almonds. Lee, a trained horticulturalist who nurtures an extensive herb garden, enjoyed a similar lovage soup in a restaurant that specialised in traditional English recipes. She then set about recreating it. Only the leaves that are tender and young should be used as, when mature, they are very bitter. The plant, which resembles giant cow parsley, grows as tall as 6-8ft!

TIP: If you don't want to nurture a friendly triffid in your garden, English Country Herbs (tel: 01284 850050) can send you fresh, seasonal herbs quickly and cheaply by post.

SERVES: 4
PREPARATION AND COOKING TIME: 40 minutes
25g (1oz) butter
1 medium onion, finely chopped
110g (4oz) fresh young lovage leaves, roughly chopped
1.2 litres (2 pints) vegetable stock (see page 14)
845 ml (1½ pints) milk
225g (8oz) ground almonds
salt and freshly ground white pepper

TO GARNISH:
150ml (¼ pint) single cream
4 dessertspoons flaked almonds, toasted

Melt the butter and cook the onion gently in a covered saucepan until soft, without colouring. Stir in the lovage, cover and cook gently for 3 minutes. Add the stock, milk and ground almonds. Cover, bring to the boil and simmer gently for 15 minutes, stirring from time to time. Cool a little, then purée in a liquidiser until smooth. Taste for seasoning. Cool, then chill in the fridge. Serve garnished with a swirl of cream and sprinkled generously with toasted flaked almonds. The soup is also delicious hot.

Smoky Fish & Fennel Chowder (F)

Anne Pearson, a food technology teacher, who lives on the edge of Derbyshire's Peak District, likes hearty soups that are thick enough to 'stand your spoon up in', so chowders are a particular favourite of hers. As a working mother with 4 children, she is always experimenting with healthy ideas for feeding large families. Anne grows fennel in her garden and she particularly likes the way that fish and fennel complement each other so well. This chunky, comforting soup is practically a meal in itself. Serve with slabs of warm granary bread or spoon on a generous helping of mashed potato to satisfy the hungriest mouths at your table.

SERVES: 4
PREPARATION AND COOKING TIME: 45 minutes

25g (1oz) butter
1 medium onion, finely sliced
1 head of fennel, about 225g (8oz), finely sliced, reserving the fennel fronds for decoration
1 teaspoon fennel seeds
½ teaspoon turmeric
1 bay leaf
225g (8oz) potato, peeled and diced small
Juice and grated rind of ½ lemon
1 rounded tablespoon Dijon mustard
225g (8oz) smoked cod or haddock
425ml (3/4 pint) milk
150ml (1/4 pint) water or dry white wine
1 dessertspoon plain flour
2 tablespoons Greek yoghurt
salt and freshly ground black pepper

TO GARNISH:
2 tablespoons fresh flat leaf parsley, finely chopped
or three or four fennel fronds per person

Melt the butter and cook the onion, fennel, fennel seeds, turmeric and bay leaf gently for 10 minutes in a covered saucepan, without colouring. Add the potato, mustard and lemon rind and cook for 2 minutes. Lay the fish on top of the vegetables and pour over the milk and water or wine. Bring to the boil, turn down heat and simmer gently, covered, for a further 10 minutes. Take the pan off the heat.

Remove and flake the fish into a separate bowl. Mix the flour and yoghurt to a paste and stir into the soup, along with lemon juice. Season carefully. Bring back to the boil, stirring continuously. Serve garnished with chopped parsley, or fennel fronds.

Swede, Turnip & Parsnip Soup

(V) (F)

Plain boiled swedes, turnips and parsnips can be rather boring, awakening memories of dreadful watery school meals. This sophisticated soup firmly places these versatile root vegetables in a different league. Alison Adcock, our Recipe Development Manager, was inspired after ordering a timbale of the three mashed together in a smart London restaurant. It reminded her how good they were together and a lovely, warming soup joined our winter range.

TIP: Always buy carrots that have their green leafy tops, they will be tastier.

SERVES : 4
PREPARATION AND COOKING TIME : 35 minutes

25g (1oz) butter
1 medium onion, finely chopped
2 medium carrots, roughly chopped
225g (8oz) swede, peeled and roughly chopped
175g (6oz) turnip, peeled and roughly chopped
150g (5oz) parsnip, peeled and roughly chopped
725ml (1¼ pints) vegetable stock (see page 14)
nutmeg, freshly grated
salt and freshly ground black pepper
100ml (4 floz) double cream

TO GARNISH :
crispy onions (see page 142)

Melt the butter and cook the onion, carrot, swede, turnip and parsnip gently for about 10 minutes in a covered saucepan, without colouring. Add the vegetable stock and season with a little nutmeg, salt and pepper. Cover, bring to the boil and simmer gently for about 15-20 minutes or until the vegetables are tender. Cool a little, then purée in a liquidiser until very smooth. Add the cream. Adjust seasoning and reheat gently. Serve garnished with crispy onions.

Rosemary's Avocado with Consommé

This very rich, dark and chilled consommé, set over freshly mashed avocado, looks as unusual as it tastes. When Rosemary Toller passed this recipe on to her son Hugh, she had no idea that it would be so popular at his frequent dinner parties. It is so good that it even saved the evening once when he forgot to invite any other men, leaving himself alone to entertain 9 women! Julia Laflin, one of our PR team, who was at the party, subsequently married Hugh and still loves this starter.

TIP: If you are in a hurry, you can cheat and use a tin of good consommé.

SERVES: 2-3
PREPARATION AND COOKING TIME: 4 hours
340g (12oz) shin of beef, cubed into 2cm (1") pieces
½ small chicken carcass, roughly chopped
1.5 litres (2½ pints) beef stock (see page 11)
1 medium onion, peeled and roughly chopped
2 carrots, peeled and roughly chopped
large sprig parsley
2 sprigs fresh thyme
1 bay leaf
6 peppercorns
1 eggshell and white of an egg
1 tablespoon dry sherry
2 avocados
2 tablespoons extra virgin olive oil
salt and pepper to taste

TO GARNISH:
1 dessertspoon fresh parsley, finely chopped

Put the beef, chicken, stock, vegetables, herbs and peppercorns into a saucepan, bring to the boil then turn down the heat and simmer uncovered for 1½-1¾ hours until reduced by approximately half. Strain and return to the heat. Beat the egg white until frothy, then whisk into the stock and add the egg shell. Reduce the heat to low and simmer for 20 minutes. This begins the clarification of the consommé. Add the sherry in the last 5 minutes. Remove from the heat and leave to cool a little. Pour through a sieve double lined with muslin. The consommé will now be clear. Cut the avocados in half, remove the stones and scoop the flesh into a bowl. Add the olive oil and mash to a smooth paste. Season with salt and pepper. Spoon the avocado into ramekins. Carefully pour the consommé into the ramekins, covering the avocado. Place the ramekins in the refrigerator for approximately 1 hour until set. Serve chilled garnished with parsley and accompanied by Melba Toast.

Autumn Ragoût of Roots & Lamb

The Henry Doubleday Research Association (HDRA) carries out research into, and promotes interest in, organic gardening, farming and food in the UK. Its Heritage Seed Library, which we have sponsored for 3 years, preserves rare, illegal and endangered varieties of vegetables to prevent their extinction. Under its 'Adopt a Veg' scheme, subscribers can choose their own unusual variety to grow and they then receive advice on how to nurture it. HDRA is based at Ryton Organic Gardens in Warwickshire, where members of the public can see its work first-hand and eat at its famed organic restaurant.

This simple, stew-like soup is served at the Ryton Organic Gardens Restaurant. The quality and varieties of vegetables used enhance the flavour. Unless you are lucky enough to be able to get all the vegetable types mentioned, we suggest you use the best organic ones you can find.

TIP: To find out how to join the Henry Doubleday Research Association, call on 01203 303617

SERVES: 6
PREPARATION AND COOKING TIME: 1 hour 15 minutes
30ml (2 tablespoons) olive oil
2 medium leeks, finely sliced
¼ swede, scrubbed, unpeeled and cut into 2.5cm (1") cubes
1 parsnip, scrubbed, unpeeled and cut into 2.5cm (1") cubes
375g (13oz) pumpkin, peeled, deseeded and cut into 2.5cm (1") cubes
175g (6oz) potato, scrubbed, unpeeled and cut into 2.5cm (1") cubes
¼ Savoy cabbage, shredded
1 salsify, scrubbed, peeled and sliced
1 carrot, scrubbed, unpeeled and sliced
375g (13oz) lamb neck fillet, cubed in 1cm (½") pieces
1.75 litres (3 pints) vegetable stock (see page 14)
2 tablespoons fresh parsley, chopped
1 tablespoon fresh marjoram, chopped
1 teaspoon fresh thyme, chopped
110g (4oz) red lentils
salt and freshly ground black pepper

VEGETABLE VARIETIES USED FROM
THE HERITAGE SEED LIBRARY:
Leeks - St Victor
Swede - Marion
Parsnip - Tender and True (1897)
Pumpkin - Turk's Turban
Potatoes - Pink Fir Apple (1850)
Savoy Cabbage - Ormskirk (1899)
Salsify - Sandwich Island
Carrot - Autumn King

Place a large, heavy bottomed saucepan over a medium heat, add the olive oil, then add the leeks and sauté for 2-3 minutes, without colouring. Add the remaining vegetables and the lamb, stir well and sauté for 5 more minutes. Pour in the stock, bring to the boil, then turn down to a simmer. Add the herbs and lentils and cook slowly, uncovered, for 35-40 minutes. Add more stock if necessary. Season to taste and serve with a dumpling of your choice.

Brown Ale, Mushroom & Lentil Soup

One of our competition finalists, Colin Brown from Wales, explained the development of this soup of his as combining his two passions - eating and drinking - in a bowl. Thane Prince, the Daily Telegraph's WEEKEND COOK, who helped us with the judging, instantly proclaimed it to be 'blokes' soup' when she tasted it.

Colin has been fascinated by cooking since childhood. He remembers that the ability to produce something edible from a collection of ingredients seemed to him to be akin to alchemy. This recipe has evolved over a number of years, the most recent modification being the addition of porcini mushrooms.

SERVES: 4
PREPARATION AND COOKING TIME: 1 hour 20 minutes

FOR THE STOCK:
1-2 litres (2 pints) water
1 small onion, halved
1 leek top, washed
1 carrot, peeled and sliced
2 sticks celery, roughly chopped
1 bay leaf
6 peppercorns

FOR THE SOUP:
2 tablespoons extra virgin olive oil
1 medium onion, finely chopped
2 garlic cloves, crushed
2 tablespoons tomato purée
50g (2oz) brown lentils, washed in plenty of cold water
110g (4oz) chestnut mushrooms, finely sliced
110g (4oz) flat mushrooms, finely sliced
15g (½oz) dried cèpe or porcini mushrooms, soaked in
    200ml (⅓ pint) warm water for 20 minutes, drained,
    reserving soaking liquor, and roughly chopped
275ml (½ pint) brown ale
dash of Worcestershire sauce (optional)

Put the stock ingredients into a saucepan. Cover, bring to the boil and simmer gently for 30 minutes. Strain into a bowl.

Heat the oil and cook the onion over a moderate heat until beginning to brown. Reduce the heat, add the garlic and cook gently for 2 minutes. Stir in the tomato purée and lentils, then the flat and chestnut mushrooms. Increase the heat and cook for 5 minutes. Stir in the brown ale and 850ml (1½ pints) of the strained stock. Cover, bring to the boil and simmer gently for 30 minutes. Add both the reconstituted cèpe and their soaking liquor to the pan, bring back to the boil and simmer for a further 10 minutes. If including Worcestershire sauce, add. Taste for seasoning and serve.

Irish Clam Chowder

The Ralston family love to sail their 58ft Nordia boat which they bought a couple of years ago and sailed back home to Northern Ireland from Holland. After one sailing trip, Lynne Ralston was given a mass of small scallops and turned them into this fantastic fishy chowder for her family of 5. The predominant flavours of this lovely creamy soup are the scallops and the sweetcorn, with the honey adding a hint of sweetness. If you have already cast your eyes over the list of ingredients and wondered, as we did at first, where the clams are, the answer is that in Ireland little scallops are known colloquially as clams or queenies.

SERVES: 6
COOKING AND PREPARATION TIME: 45 minutes

14 medium scallops, chopped into quarters, or 500g (1lb 2oz) small queen scallops, adding corals if preferred
2 small young leeks, sliced very finely
1 large potato, peeled and diced
2 rashers smoked streaky bacon, sliced finely
340g (12oz) frozen sweetcorn
200g (7oz) crème fraîche
275ml (10 floz) single cream
570ml (1 pint) fish or vegetable stock (see page 13 or 14)
50g (2oz) butter, preferably unsalted
1 level teaspoon honey
1 heaped dessertspoon plain flour
Salt and freshly ground black pepper

TO GARNISH:
fresh parsley, chopped

Sauté leeks, potato and bacon in butter for about 20 minutes until soft. Add 3/4 of the stock and cook for 10 minutes, then add the sweetcorn.

Mix the flour with the remaining stock, add to the saucepan and heat until warmed through. Add the crème fraîche, cream and chopped scallops. Heat gently until the scallops are firm. Be careful not to cook too quickly or for too long or they will become tough.

Add honey just before serving and season to taste. Sprinkle with fresh parsley and serve with hot fresh crusty bread.

Parsnip, Leek & Lemon Soup

(V) (F)

This sweet and tangy soup is made for those dark winter months when the ground is frozen and the few vegetables growing are stiff and rimmed with hoarfrost. Part-time doctor, livestock breeder and mother of 4, Elizabeth Ffrench-Constant entered this soup in one of our 'Create a Soup' competitions, having invented it to use up a glut of leeks from her husband's vegetable plot. Smooth and satisfying, this soup is just right for a winter's day, but do also try it cold.

TIP: Parsnips and other root vegetables are at their sweetest and best after the first frost of winter, which converts their starch content into sugar.

SERVES: 4
PREPARATION AND COOKING TIME: 35 minutes
25g (1oz) butter
450g (1lb) parsnips, peeled and sliced
3 leeks, washed well and sliced
1 litre (1¾ pints) vegetable stock (see page 14)
grated rind and juice of ½ lemon
1 bay leaf
150ml (¼ pint) single cream
salt

Melt the butter and cook the parsnips and leeks for 5 minutes in a covered saucepan, without colouring. Add the vegetable stock, grated lemon rind and bay leaf. Bring to the boil and simmer gently for about 15 minutes until the vegetables are tender. Cool a little, remove the bay leaf, and add the lemon juice. Purée thoroughly in a liquidiser until very smooth. Add the cream, taste for seasoning and reheat, but do not boil.

Plum Soup

Rhianon Evans's mother used to make this slightly tart plum soup with ripe fruit from the orchard of the family's farm in Wales. One day, on a whim, we poured squiggles of hot melted chocolate and double cream over a bowlful. The chocolate set when it hit the cold soup and the result looked and tasted delectable. The contrast of sweet and sour, smooth and hard, really needs to be tasted to be believed. A perfect 'summer pud for using up some of the plums from your garden.

SERVES: 4
PREPARATION AND COOKING TIME: 40 minutes
675g (1½lb) red plums
a little water
290ml (½ pint) good red wine
2 tablespoons lemon juice
pinch of ground cloves
½ teaspoon mixed spice
about 4 tablespoons sugar (to taste)
I level tablespoon cornflour
290ml (½ pint) buttermilk

TO GARNISH:
75g (3oz) plain chocolate, melted in a bowl over a
              pan of simmering water
100ml (4 floz) double cream

Put the plums into a saucepan with a little water. Cover and simmer for about 10-15 minutes or until tender. Pass the plums and juices through a sieve into a clean saucepan and add the red wine, lemon juice, ground cloves, mixed spice and sugar to taste. Mix the cornflour with a little water until smooth and stir into the soup until well incorporated. Bring to the boil, stirring until the mixture thickens and simmer gently for 2 minutes. Allow the soup to cool, stir in the buttermilk, then chill well. Serve the soup garnished with swirls of melted plain chocolate and double cream.

Celeriac Soup with Green Herbs & Lime

As Head of Art and Design at La Sagesse High School in Newcastle-upon-Tyne, Hilary Ketchin is constantly searching for new ideas. She gets as excited about her cooking as she does about art and design. What she loves most is the challenge of awakening tastebuds to new combinations of ingredients and flavours.

This celeriac creation was composed by Hilary on a damp summer's day, the kind of day when you plan to eat in the garden with friends, but the weather renders you housebound. Perfect for unpredictable weather, it's just as delicious served chilled outside, or heated, indoors.

SERVES: 6
PREPARATION TIME: 25 minutes   COOKING TIME: 30 minutes

2 tablespoons groundnut oil
900g (2lb) celeriac, peeled and roughly chopped
1.75 litres (3 pints) chicken stock (see page 9)
Juice 1 lime
2.5cm (1") fresh ginger, grated
1 teaspoon lemon thyme, freshly chopped
1 green chilli, seeded and chopped
small bunch of fresh coriander, leaves and stalks separated
75g (3oz) creamed coconut block
salt

TO GARNISH:
4 spring onions, chopped

Heat the oil and cook the celeriac gently in a covered saucepan for 10 minutes, without colouring. Add the stock, lime juice, ginger, lemon thyme, chopped chilli and coriander stems. Bring to the boil and simmer, covered, for 30 minutes until the vegetables are tender. Remove from the heat and add the creamed coconut. Cool a little, then purée in a liquidiser until smooth. Taste for seasoning. Reheat gently, stir in most of the chopped coriander leaves and serve the soup sprinkled with the remaining herbs and spring onions.

Three Onion Soup

When we first produced our own version of a French onion soup, we never dreamt that, like taking coals to Newcastle, it would become popular in France. Over the years, we have been fortunate enough to have many variations of this classic recipe sent to us, but when we tried this version we were fascinated. The sweetness of red onions, the strength of shallots and the colour of spring onions combine beautifully in this superior onion soup, while chicken, rather than beef, stock gives a rich and interesting flavour. This is a must for anyone passionate about onions.

TIP: Greek yoghurt and double cream are better for stirring into hot food than natural yoghurt or single cream. The latter 2 have a lower fat content and are therefore more likely to curdle.

SERVES: 4
PREPARATION AND COOKING TIME: 1 hour 30 minutes

4 tablespoons extra virgin olive oil
750g (1lb 11oz) red onions, finely sliced
340g (12oz) shallots, finely sliced
3 teaspoons plain flour
2 teaspoons mustard
1·2 litres (2 pints) chicken stock (see page 9)
4 sprigs of fresh thyme
3 tablespoons Greek yoghurt
salt and freshly ground black pepper

TO GARNISH:
1 bunch spring onions, finely sliced

Heat the oil and fry the red onions and shallots over a moderate heat, stirring, for 20-30 minutes until golden and caramelised. Stir in the flour and mustard and cook gently for 2 minutes. Add the stock and thyme, then bring to the boil, stirring well. Cover and simmer for 30 minutes, remove from heat and pick out the thyme sprigs. Stir in the yoghurt and taste for seasoning. Serve the soup scattered liberally with sliced spring onions.

Asparagus & Roasted Garlic Soup (V) (F)

Garlic is well known for its blood purifying properties as well as its fabled ability to deter vampires. Purely co-incidentally, Michele Platman, who sent us this recipe, is mad about garlic and works for the National Blood Service! Whenever she follows a recipe requiring one clove of garlic she always doubles or trebles it, so beware, this is not a recipe for the faint-hearted!

Michele goes to Judy Goodman's famous goose farm at Great Witley in Worcestershire in the asparagus season and buys bagfuls of soup grade spears for her freezer, generously sold for a handful of pennies. Michele's experiments with the asparagus and her beloved garlic resulted in this sensational luxurious and creamy soup.

TIP: Use the left-over oil from roasting the garlic for cooking or to flavour salad dressing.

SERVES: 4
PREPARATION AND COOKING TIME: previous day - 40 minutes; same day - 60 minutes
Pre-heat the oven to 180°C / 350°F / Gas Mark 4

1 large glass jar
3 heads of garlic
570ml (1 pint) extra virgin olive oil
3 large sprigs of fresh rosemary
1 medium onion, finely sliced
450g (1lb) good fresh asparagus, if using older stringy asparagus
        double the quantity, cut into 5cm (2") pieces
1 tablespoon plain flour
850ml (1½ pints) vegetable stock (see page 14)
salt and freshly ground white pepper
150 ml (¼ pint) single cream

TO GARNISH:
2 tablespoons fresh flat leaf parsley, chopped
zest of 1 lemon, grated
1 quantity garlic croûtons (see page 142)

Sterilise a large glass jar by putting a clean jar in the oven for 10 minutes. Take out of the oven and allow to cool.

To roast the garlic, remove only excess papery skin from the garlic heads and put them into a small baking tin with 3 tablespoons of the olive oil. Roast for 15-20 minutes until soft. Remove from the oven and allow to cool. Trim off the top 1cm (½") of the garlic heads. Pack the garlic and sprigs of rosemary into the sterilised jar and completely cover the garlic with the remaining olive oil. Seal the jar and leave overnight.

Heat 4 tablespoons of the olive oil from the jar and cook the onion gently in a covered saucepan for 5 minutes. Peel and finely chop 4 cloves of the preserved garlic and add to the pan. Cook gently for a further 5 minutes, without colouring. Add the asparagus and cook gently for 2 minutes. Stir in the flour and cook gently for 2 minutes. Gradually add the stock, stirring all the time. Cover, bring to the boil and simmer gently for about 15-20 minutes until the asparagus is tender. Cool a little, then purée in a liquidiser until very smooth. Pass through a fine sieve to remove any stringy fibres. Add the cream and reheat gently but do not boil as this will curdle the soup. Season to taste. Serve garnished with chopped parsley, lemon zest and garlic croûtons. This soup is delicious chilled too.

Tomato & Basil Vichyssoise (V) (F)

This is our variation of Vichyssoise, a leek and potato soup traditionally thickened with cream and served cold. Vichyssoise was the invention of master chef Louis Diat, who was persuaded by César Ritz to work at his famous hotels in London, Paris and New York. Diat based his recipe on the French classic 'potage à la bonne femme', but he served his version cold. Ever since, the name Vichyssoise has been given to many cold soups based on potato and another vegetable. Our leek and potato Vichyssoise has been one of our top-selling soups ever since we first started making soup. This variation is becoming just as popular.

SERVES: 4
PREPARATION AND COOKING TIME: 30 minutes
25g (1oz) butter
1 small onion, finely chopped
1 large leek, washed and finely sliced
225g (8oz) potato, peeled and roughly chopped
860ml (1½ pints) vegetable stock (see page 14)
75g (3oz) tinned chopped plum tomatoes
50g (2oz) tomato purée
275ml (½ pint) milk
2 tablespoons fresh basil, chopped
salt and freshly ground black pepper

TO GARNISH:
150ml (¼ pint) sour cream
finely pared peel 1 orange
or
ice cubes
fresh Parmesan cheese shavings

Melt the butter and cook the onion and leek gently for 5 minutes in a covered saucepan, without colouring. Add the potato and vegetable stock. Taste for seasoning. Cover, bring to the boil and simmer gently for about 10 minutes until the potato is tender. Add the tinned tomatoes and tomato purée and cook gently for a further 3 minutes. Cool a little then purée in a liquidiser until very smooth. Return to a clean saucepan and stir in the milk and chopped fresh basil. Adjust the seasoning and chill. Serve garnished with a spoonful of sour cream and slivers of finely pared orange peel or with ice cubes and shavings of fresh Parmesan cheese. You can also serve it warm.

Celeriac & Porcini Soup

V F

A luxurious, rich and elegant treat, this soup is the brainchild of talented cook Valerie Ison, whom we met at the final of one of our soup competitions. We still remember the spine-chilling conversations we had with her husband over dinner that night. As an ex-Scotland Yard man turned crime writer, he certainly had a fascinating tale or two to tell!

SERVES: 4
PREPARATION AND COOKING TIME: 45 minutes
50g (2oz) butter
1 medium onion, finely chopped
110g (4oz) celeriac, peeled and roughly chopped
15g (½oz) dried porcini/cèpe mushrooms, soaked for
              20 minutes with 150ml (¼ pint) boiling water
290ml (½ pint) water
200ml (7 floz) crème fraîche
1 tablespoon fresh dill, chopped
salt and freshly ground black pepper

TO GARNISH:
plain croûtons (see page 142 follow the recipe for garlic croûtons omitting the garlic).

Melt the butter and cook the onion and celeriac gently for 10 minutes in a covered saucepan, without colouring. Strain the porcini soaking liquor into the pan, chop the porcini and add to the pan. Add the water, cover, bring to the boil and simmer gently for about 15 minutes or until the vegetables are tender. Cool a little, then purée in a liquidiser until very smooth.

Stir in the crème fraîche and dill and taste for seasoning. Reheat gently, and garnish with croûtons.

French Clear Fish Bouillabaisse

When Reinhard Adam started his 3 year training as a chef at the Martim Hotel in Timmendorf, he was faced with the problem of how to serve Bouillabaisse to German customers who did not like cloudy soups. His solution was to use clear fish stock.

Reinhard then moved to London, where he worked in some of the capital's best-known restaurants. To spend more time with his family, he joined Europa Foods, who sell over 1 million cartons of our fresh soup every year through their London chain of convenience stores.

Bouillabaisse describes a method of cooking rather than an actual recipe. There are as many 'authentic' bouillabaisses as there are ways of combining fish. This recipe uses an extravagant collection. The flavour is so marvellous that a garnish is not necessary - just mop up the juices with some good bread.

TIP: It is important not to overcook the vegetables or the fish. Putting the fish into the hot stock and bringing it almost to the boil is sufficient to cook it through. Always remove fish from the refrigerator and allow to come up to room temperature before cooking.

SERVES: 4
PREPARATION AND COOKING TIME: 35 minutes
1 tablespoon sunflower oil
1 red onion, finely sliced
1 leek, white only, finely sliced
2 carrots, cut into fine strips
a pinch of saffron threads
1 litre (1 3/4 pints) clear fish stock (see page 13)
2 tablespoons fresh flat leaf parsley, chopped
2 teaspoons fresh dill, chopped
Pernod to taste (approx. a capful)
110g (4oz) fresh skinned salmon fillet, cut into 1cm (½") strips
110g (4oz) fresh skinned lemon sole fillet, cut into 1cm (½") strips
110g (4oz) fresh skinned turbot fillet, cut into 1cm (½") strips
60g (2½oz) cooked shelled prawns
60g (2½oz) cooked shelled mussels
60g (2½oz) scallops, trimmed of the white muscle
salt and freshly ground black pepper

Heat the oil and fry the vegetables until golden, about 10 minutes. Stir in the saffron and fish stock. Cover, bring to the boil and simmer gently for 10 minutes.

Stir the parsley, dill and a little dash of Pernod into the soup. Add the fish and stir gently. Taste for seasoning. Bring almost to the boil very carefully and do not stir as this may break up the fish. Serve warm.

Roasted Garlic Vichyssoise

Craig Nash, from County Down, decided to take a classic soup and 'jazz it up' for his entry in one of our annual 'Create a Soup' competitions. He made it to the final – his idea of enhancing Vichyssoise with roasted garlic was brilliant.

At the dinner the night before the cook-off, Craig realised in conversation that one of his old friends from Cambridge was our Managing Director. Not wanting to be accused of having swayed the result, he didn't let on until afterwards.

A delicious soup, it's not as potent as it sounds – roasting the whole bulb of garlic has a mellowing effect. Smooth and creamy, it can be served hot or chilled.

SERVES: 8
PREPARATION AND COOKING TIME: 40 minutes
Pre-heat the oven to 170°C/325°F/Gas Mark 3

1 head of garlic, separated into unpeeled cloves
100ml (4 floz) extra virgin olive oil
150g (5oz) butter
4 leeks, washed and roughly chopped
900g (2lb) Maris Piper, or similar, potatoes,
              peeled and roughly chopped
1.2 litres (2 pints) chicken stock (see page 9)
150ml (¼ pint) double cream
salt and freshly ground black pepper

TO GARNISH:
2 tablespoons fresh chives, snipped

Toss the garlic in the olive oil in a small ovenproof dish, cover and roast for 15-20 minutes until soft. Remove from the oven and leave to cool. Meanwhile, melt the butter and cook the leeks for 10 minutes over a moderate heat in a covered saucepan until beginning to wilt but without colouring, stirring frequently. Add the potatoes and chicken stock. Cover, bring to the boil and simmer gently for about 15 minutes until the vegetables are tender. Peel the garlic and add to the soup. Cool a little, then purée in a liquidiser until very smooth. Transfer to a clean saucepan and stir in the double cream and, if necessary, a little water to thin to the required consistency. Taste for seasoning. Reheat gently and serve garnished with snipped fresh chives.

Champagne Soup

Moira Cook, a good friend and lover of fine food, adores champagne and was given this recipe by an extravagant friend when she first had a flat in London. At the time, Moira's cooking skills were non-existent, but she had high hopes of entertaining on a grand scale. Her father advised her that anything she attempted to cook should always contain alcohol, and preferably be flambéd, in order to disguise what was inevitably going to taste atrocious. Moira discovered that his advice was excellent, although it was not, sadly, accompanied by crates of his recommended ingredients. This solid champagne pudding soup has proved to be the most popular of all. As it delivers a kick powerful enough to defrost the stuffiest dinner guest, it is advisable to be sitting down when eating it.

SERVES: 6-8
PREPARATION TIME: 10 minutes   **COOKING TIME:** 45 minutes

Pre-heat the oven to 150°C / 300°F / Gas Mark 2

1 bottle pink champagne
1 cinnamon stick
10 egg yolks
8 tablespoons caster sugar
2 tablespoons icing sugar

Heat the champagne and cinnamon stick almost to boiling point. Do not boil or you will lose the alcohol.

Meanwhile, whisk the egg yolks and sugar until thick and pale. Put into a bowl and gradually stir in the very hot champagne. Pass through a fine sieve into a large wide measuring jug. Put ramekins into a roasting tin and pour the champagne mixture into them. Place in the oven, pour boiling water into the roasting tin, avoiding the ramekins, to a depth of 2.5 cms (1") and bake for about 40 minutes until set. Take the ramekins out of the roasting tin and allow to cool. Chill well. Serve with a liberal dusting of icing sugar.

Minestra di Farro e Fagioli
(Bean & Spelt Soup)

(V)

Ornella de Gennaro is descended from an ancient line of dukes originating from the Molise region of Southern Italy. Her sister still lives there in an old family round tower. Spelt grain and flour was widely used in Italy during Roman times and Ornella's ancestors and relations have been cooking this recipe at home for as long as anybody can remember. This is an easy soup to make and the result - beans and grains in a broth flavoured with rosemary, sage and garlic - is rustic in character and very satisfying. Like all bean soups, it is better made the day before you eat it, to allow the flavours to develop

Spelt grain is hard to come by in Britain. Italian delicatessens or specialist health food shops stock it or may be prepared to order in the Crazy Jack brand. Alternatively, buy some on your next Italian holiday!

TIP: from the de Gennaro family Kitchen - try adding a spoonful of pesto to any vegetable soup before serving.

SERVES: 4
PREPARATION AND COOKING TIME:
overnight soaking of the beans and spelt grain
plus 1 hour 10 minutes

250g (9oz) borlotti beans ⎫ soaked together in a bowl
150g (5oz) spelt grain ⎭ overnight with plenty of cold water.
(Alternatively, soak for 2 hours before cooking and be
prepared to cook for a little longer)

1 tablespoon extra virgin olive oil
10 medium to large fresh sage leaves
5 sprigs fresh rosemary
2 garlic cloves, peeled but left whole
2 litres (3½ pints) vegetable stock (see page 14)
freshly ground black pepper
salt
a little extra olive oil for serving

Rinse and drain the beans and spelt. Put into a saucepan with the oil, sage, rosemary, garlic, stock and a little pepper. Bring to the boil and then simmer very gently uncovered for about 1 hour, or until the beans and spelt are tender. Add salt to taste.

Remove sage, rosemary and garlic and pour into individual dishes, each containing a little olive oil.

Red Onion &
Roasted Cherry Tomato Soup

Ⓥ Ⓕ

Kathryn Kenworthy's rich, red soup was inspired by her honeymoon in Italy, where she and her husband spent many hours ambling through markets, choosing the freshest vegetables and local produce. Kathryn particularly loves the simplicity of Mediterranean food. She describes her soup as 'a marriage of her love of onions and her husband's passion for tomatoes'.

This soup uses cherry tomatoes rather extravagantly, but is also delicious with any sweet, juicy, full-flavoured, home-grown or Italian tomatoes.

SERVES: 4
PREPARATION AND COOKING TIME: 1 hour 20 minutes

Pre-heat the oven to 190°C/375°F/Gas Mark 5

1·35Kg (3lb) cherry tomatoes
3 large garlic cloves, quartered
3 red onions - 2 finely sliced, 1 chopped
1 large handful of fresh basil leaves
approximately 4 tablespoons olive oil
25g (1oz) butter
2 teaspoons balsamic vinegar
2 heaped teaspoons dark brown sugar
Salt and freshly ground black pepper
300ml (11floz) boiling water

TO GARNISH:
halved cherry tomatoes
basil leaves
or Pesto Croûtons (see page 143)

Place the cherry tomatoes into a shallow roasting tin, along with the garlic cloves and the chopped onion. Scatter half a dozen basil leaves in the tin and season with salt and pepper. Coat well with ¾ of the olive oil and roast for approximately 50-60 minutes, until the tomatoes are soft and beginning to brown. Melt the butter and gently fry the remaining onions until they are tender and caramelised. After about 10 minutes, add the balsamic vinegar and the sugar to the onions and cook for another 2 minutes.

Purée the cooked tomatoes in a liquidiser with a little water and pass through a fine sieve. Add the purée and any remaining water to the onions and taste for seasoning. Tear the remaining basil leaves and stir into the soup. Reheat gently and serve garnished with the halves of cherry tomato and basil leaves or with pesto croûtons.

Tomato, Spinach & Mascarpone Soup

(V) (F)

Mascarpone cheese is so light and creamy that cookery writer Elizabeth David used to spread it on homemade bread in place of butter. Because of its lightness it is the ideal ingredient for a chilled summer soup. Combined with the fresh flavours of tomatoes and spinach, it doesn't give the claggy heaviness you find in some cheese soups. The taste is clean and the appearance pretty - reddish in colour with dark flecks of spinach.

SERVES: 4
PREPARATION TIME: 10 minutes
COOKING TIME: 40 minutes

25g (1oz) butter
1 medium onion, finely chopped
1 garlic clove, crushed
1 medium potato, about 200g (7oz) roughly chopped
570ml (1 pint) vegetable stock (see page 14)
400g (14oz) fresh tomatoes, roughly chopped
1 dessertspoon tomato purée
170g (6oz) fresh spinach
1 tablespoon freshly grated Parmesan cheese
3 tablespoons mascarpone cheese
Salt and freshly ground black pepper
150ml (¼ pint) milk

TO GARNISH:
2 tomatoes, diced
4 sprigs of fresh basil

Melt the butter and cook the onion and garlic gently in a covered saucepan for 10 minutes, without colouring. Add the potato and stock. Cover, bring to the boil, and simmer gently for about 20 minutes until the vegetables are tender. Cool a little, then purée in a liquidiser until smooth. Add the remaining ingredients, cover, bring to the boil and simmer gently for a further 15 minutes. Serve garnished with tomato dice and sprigs of fresh basil.

Aubergine Soup with Mint & Pine Nuts

(V) (F)

There's no escape from aubergines and white beans in Greek tavernas, as Gill Lewis discovered on her numerous Greek holidays. Inspired by these ingredients, Gill created this chunky, rustic-style soup. All the different flavours come through as you eat it, while the mint and pine nut garnish really finishes it off. It is so good that when we came to test it for the book there was a great deal of competitive spoon jostling as we fought to finish the bowl!

SERVES: 4
PREPARATION TIME: 25 minutes
COOKING TIME: 45 minutes
Pre-heat the oven to 200°C/400°F/Gas Mark 6

2 large aubergines, about 700g (1lb 9oz)
3 tablespoons extra virgin olive oil
1 shallot, chopped
1 garlic clove, crushed
½ level teaspoon ground cumin
½ level teaspoon ground cinnamon
3 large plum tomatoes, skinned and chopped
150g (5oz) cooked butter beans
salt and freshly ground black pepper
500ml (17½ fl oz) vegetable stock (see page 14)
        or the bean cooking water

TO GARNISH:
2 tablespoons mint, chopped
2 tablespoons pine nuts, toasted

Put the aubergines into a large saucepan and cover with boiling water. Simmer for 10 minutes, then drain and cut in half lengthways. Slash the cut sides in 3 places and brush with 2 tablespoons of the olive oil. Put onto a baking sheet and bake for 10 minutes. Remove from the oven and cool. Remove the skins and cut the flesh into 2.5cm (1") dice.

While the aubergines are cooking, heat the remaining olive oil and cook the shallot and garlic gently in a covered saucepan for 5 minutes, without colouring. Stir in the cumin and cinnamon and cook for a further 2 minutes. Add the chopped tomatoes, diced aubergine and butter beans. Taste for seasoning. Cook for 2 minutes. Add the stock, cover, bring to the boil and simmer for 20 minutes until tender. Cool a little, then blend for 1 second in a food processor or roughly chop in the pan with kitchen scissors. Thin if necessary with a little more liquid. Heat through and serve liberally sprinkled with chopped fresh mint and toasted pine nuts.

Cream of Turnip Soup with Lime & Bacon

East meets West in this unusual soup by Alison Burt, who wrote ten cookery books for Hamlyn when she lived in Australia. She returned to England to set up 'Alison & Kate's' restaurant with her sister in Westerham, Kent in 1977. It was full every night for the 10 years they ran it before deciding to throw in the teatowel. It was so successful that Alison, who now has a flourishing catering company, is still asked to produce many of its popular recipes. Alison invented this recipe full of good, strong flavours especially for us. (It's actually made with smoked ham but we've used the word bacon in its wider sense!)

TIP: chilli sauces vary in heat and quality. One readily available sauce we recommend is Walkers Wood 'Seriously Hot Jamaican Jon Kanoo Pepper Sauce'.

SERVES: 4
PREPARATION AND COOKING TIME: 1 hour 5 minutes

50g (2oz) butter
1 medium onion, finely chopped
675g (1½lbs) turnip, peeled and cut into 2.5cm (1") dice
250g (9oz) potatoes, peeled and cut into 2.5cm (1") dice
1 thick lime slice, including skin
850ml (1½pints) vegetable stock (see page 14)
2 tablespoons crème fraîche
1 teaspoon chilli sauce, or to taste
250g (9oz) smoked ham, cut into 2.5cm (·1") slivers
salt and freshly ground black pepper

TO GARNISH:
slivers of smoked ham
rind of 1 lime

Melt the butter and cook the onion, turnip, potatoes and lime in a covered saucepan for 5 minutes without colouring, stirring from time to time. Add the stock, cover and bring to the boil. Simmer gently for 30 minutes or until the vegetables are very tender. Cool a little, then purée in a liquidiser until very smooth, making sure the lime is well puréed too.

Return to a clean saucepan and stir in the crème fraîche, chilli sauce and smoked ham. Taste for seasoning. Reheat gently, stirring, and serve with a twist of freshly ground black pepper and rind, garnished with the smoked ham slivers and lime.

Broccoli Soup with Lime & Cream of Horseradish

Ⓥ Ⓕ

Angela Allright's zingy version of broccoli soup is one of those recipes you remember long after the bowl has been scraped clean. Created specially for our 1998 'Create a Soup' competition in the Daily Telegraph, cordon-bleu trained cook Angela was one of the competition's 6 finalists. This highly original combination of ingredients is light in texture, and reasonably low in fat for all those who want to watch their personal fatometers.

We prefer making it with chicken stock. It gives a better depth of flavour.

SERVES: 4
PREPARATION AND COOKING TIME : 1 hour
15g (½oz) butter
1 small onion, chopped
110g (4oz) potato, peeled and cubed
270g (10oz) broccoli, chopped
850ml (1½ pints) vegetable or chicken stock (see page 9)
1 lime, zest plus juice
2 tablespoons parsley and chives, chopped
2 teaspoons fresh horseradish, grated
2 tablespoons double cream
salt and freshly ground black pepper

TO GARNISH:
Chopped herbs
croutons

Melt the butter and cook the onion and potato gently for 5 minutes without colouring. Add the stock and the zest and juice of lime. Cover, bring to the boil and simmer gently for about 30 minutes until the vegetables are tender. Meanwhile cook the broccoli in boiling water for 10 minutes, or until tender but still green. Cool the potato mixture a little then purée in a liquidiser and pass through a sieve. Return to the liquidiser and add the cooked broccoli. Liquidise briefly so that you can still see bits of broccoli. Return to the pan and add herbs, cream, enough horseradish and seasoning to taste. Check and adjust consistency. Garnish with chopped herbs and croutons.

Tomato Borscht

When we first started making fresh soup back in 1988, we only bought vegetables in small quantities and so could buy direct from New Covent Garden Market. As we were able to use the freshest ingredients just as they came into season, we decided to produce a range of 'Soup of the Month' recipes using vegetables at their peak. Tomato Borscht is a good example.

If one recipe from Russian and Polish cookery stands out, it is the vividly coloured borscht. There are many variations of this popular recipe, some richer than others. It can include meat or any type of vegetable, but the one ingredient that gives it its typical colour and characteristics is beetroot.

Our adaptation, designed for summer eating, was the creation of Joanne Board, then a student working for us on her sandwich placement, who, like all the other placement students we have had, went on to gain a 1st class degree. Whilst she was with us, Joanne got engaged to Anthony Scott, who worked in our engineering department, so she certainly left us with more than she bargained for!

SERVES: 4
PREPARATION AND COOKING TIME: 45 minutes
25g (1oz) butter
1 small onion, finely chopped
1 garlic clove, crushed
225g (8oz) raw beetroot, grated
1 teaspoon ground cumin
½ teaspoon ground cinnamon
225g (8oz) fresh ripe tomatoes, skinned and roughly chopped
275ml (½ pint) tomato juice
1 tablespoon tomato purée
570ml (1 pint) vegetable stock (see page 14)
1 tablespoon soy sauce
salt and freshly ground black pepper

Melt the butter and cook the onion, garlic and beetroot gently in a covered saucepan for 10 minutes, without colouring. Add the cumin, cinnamon, tomatoes, tomato juice and tomato purée and stock. Cover, bring to the boil and simmer gently for about 15 minutes until the vegetables are tender. Add the soy sauce and taste for seasoning. Cool a little, then purée in a liquidiser until very smooth. Reheat gently. It is also delicious served well chilled.

Salmon & Dill Soup

John Joseph, our factory manager in London, obtained this recipe whilst backpacking around Russia with his wife, Carol. En route to Helsinki, they boarded a Finnish train in St. Petersburg and headed hungrily for the restaurant car where they were served this refined and creamy salmon soup. After weeks of dull stodge it was 'absolute nectar'. In her best pidgin Finnish, Carol asked the chef for the recipe. She never worked out if dill was the herb they used (her Finnish wasn't that good!), but it works fantastically anyway.

SERVES: 4
PREPARATION TIME : 15 minutes   COOKING TIME: 30 minutes

250ml (9 floz) double cream
2 tablespoons olive oil
1 medium onion, finely diced
570ml (1 pint) fresh vegetable stock (see page 14)
200ml (7 floz) dry white wine
450g (1lb) (approx 3) potatoes, peeled and cut into 1cm (½") dice
salt and freshly ground pepper
300g (11oz) fresh salmon (tail fillet), skinned and cut into 3.5cm (1½") chunks
1½ tablespoons dill, chopped

Remove cream from fridge and allow to come to room temperature.

Meanwhile heat oil and cook onion gently in covered saucepan for 5 minutes, without colouring. Add the stock, wine, potato and seasoning. Bring to the boil and simmer for 15 minutes without a lid, until tender but not too soft.

Add cubed salmon, bring back to the boil, add dill and remove from heat. Leave to stand for a couple of minutes. The hot stock will continue to cook the salmon.

Add cream, heat through gently without boiling and serve immediately.

Red Lentil & Butternut Pottage with Marrow Chips

(V) (F)

If apprentice chef Phil Hardie turns out to be the next Gary Rhodes, remember you read about him here first! As a latch-key kid, Phil learnt to cook and look after himself early on. He began his professional catering career by working in South Africa and then running a restaurant in the Canaries. Being ambitious, he decided that the training he would receive at Butlers' Wharf Chef School, set up by leading restaurant groups, would serve him well. In between toughing it out in the kitchen and attending demonstration sessions with successful chefs such as Brian Turner, Phil invented this brilliant soup for us. The crispy marrow chips are the perfect finishing touch.

SERVES: 4
PREPARATION AND COOKING TIME: 1 hour

FOR THE FORTIFIED STOCK:
50g (2oz) butter
1 small onion, roughly chopped
140g (5oz) carrots, roughly chopped
140g (5oz) celery, roughly chopped
425ml (3/4 pint) vegetable stock (see page 14)
570ml (1 pint) water

FOR THE SOUP:
225g (8oz) red lentils, soaked for 30 minutes and rinsed in plenty of cold water
50g (2oz) butter
1 medium onion, finely chopped
675g (1½lb) butternut squash, peeled and cut into 2.5cm (1") pieces
1 bay leaf
1 litre (1¾ pints) fortified stock (see above)
salt and freshly ground black pepper

TO GARNISH:
1 small marrow or courgette, deseeded and cut into 10cm (4") long very fine chips
150ml (¼ pint) crème fraîche
2 tablespoons fresh coriander leaves, chopped

To make the stock, melt the butter and cook the onion, carrot and celery gently in a covered saucepan for 5 minutes, without colouring. Add the stock and water. Cover, bring to the boil and simmer gently for 30 minutes. Strain into a bowl without pressing the vegetables too firmly.

To make the soup, prepare the lentils as detailed above. While they are soaking, melt the butter and cook the onion and butternut squash gently with the bay leaf for about 15 minutes in a covered saucepan, without colouring. Add the stock, the rinsed lentils and taste for seasoning. Cover, bring to the boil and simmer for about 30 minutes until the vegetables are tender. Cool a little, then purée in a liquidiser until very smooth. Adjust the seasoning and thin with a little water to the desired consistency if necessary. Reheat gently.

While reheating, deep fry the marrow chips until lightly brown and crisp. Remove from the pan to kitchen paper and sprinkle with a little salt.

Serve the soup garnished with a swirl of crème fraîche, a generous pinch of the marrow chips and a pinch of chopped fresh coriander leaves.

Spicy Tomato, Aubergine & Apricot Soup

(V)

So keen on soup is new recruit Andrea Hamilton that she gave us this recipe in her 1st week at work. Having studied food and nutrition at university, she considers cookery, eating and drinking to be her main hobbies. Eat a bowlful of her comforting but exotic soup, with its sweet and spicy flavours, and you will feel instantly transported to the Middle East.

SERVES: 6-8
PREPARATION AND COOKING TIME: 1 hour 15 minutes
Pre-heat oven to 200°C / 400°F / Gas Mark 6

675g (1½lbs) aubergines (approx 3)
6 tablespoons olive oil
1 teaspoon cumin seeds
1 medium onion, finely chopped
2 garlic cloves, finely chopped
1 red chilli, deseeded and finely chopped
110g (4oz) dried apricots (ready to use), finely chopped
2.5cm (1") piece of ginger, peeled and finely chopped
450ml (16floz) tomato passata
juice of ½ lemon
1.5 litres (2½ pints) vegetable stock (see page 14)
salt and freshly ground black pepper to taste
1 tablespoon fresh coriander leaves, chopped

TO GARNISH:
a handful of fresh coriander leaves, finely chopped

Cut the aubergines in half, brush with 3 tablespoons of the olive oil and bake for approximately 30 minutes until soft. Remove from the oven and chop roughly. Heat the remaining oil in a saucepan and sauté the cumin, onion, garlic and chilli for 2-3 minutes, without colouring. Add the apricots, ginger, passata, lemon juice, aubergines and half of the stock. Bring to the boil, then reduce the heat and simmer for 20 minutes. Leave to cool. Process in a liquidiser until smooth, then return the soup to the pan. Add the remaining stock and taste for seasoning. Stir in the coriander and serve, sprinkled with more coriander.

Chilled Melon & Ginger Soup

NiKKi Rowan Kedge and Angela Rowson put on a garden party to celebrate the end of 26 years running The Loaves & Fishes Restaurant, at which they served this sweet, yet piquant soup as a starter. It was a day to remember. NiKKi and Angela hired the local scout 'marquee', a large green ex-army supply tent - the sort in which some of their guests would have eaten and slept in Egypt or India during the 2nd World War. A clarinet trio played in the background and the sun shone. The soup is incredibly easy to make and the pale lime green colour looks terrific. It is also wonderfully refreshing at picnics on a hot summer's day. Just put it in a flask with some ice cubes, and don't forget the bunch of fresh mint.

SERVES: 4
PREPARATION AND COOKING TIME : 10 minutes

2 small full-flavoured melons, halved, pips removed
              and flesh removed from the skin
6 pieces of preserved ginger in syrup, sliced
290ml (½ pint) Greek yoghurt
2 tablespoons sugar
290ml (½ pint) single cream

TO GARNISH:
150ml (¼ pint) double cream
a few fresh mint leaves, chopped

Put the melon flesh, ginger slices, Greek yoghurt and sugar into a liquidiser and purée until very smooth. Empty into a bowl and stir in the single cream. Chill very well. To serve, ladle into bowls and top with a swirl of double cream and a sprinkling of chopped fresh mint.

Bengal Lancers' Soup

Chris Thompson, a finalist in our 1998 'Create a Soup' competition which appeared in the Daily Telegraph, regularly jets around the world as a Cabin Service Director for British Airways. A talented and accomplished cook, he describes cooking as his hobby, his interest, his relaxation and his main 'raison d'être'. He loves to talk about food, read about it, watch programmes on it, collect books on it, eat it, shop for it and has even written articles for a BA magazine about it!

His delicious dal type soup, using ingredients found in the cooking of India's West Bengal region, is thick and satisfying, but also fresh-tasting and aromatic. The soup's name, which conjures up images of pith-helmeted, khaki-clad soldiers galloping across a dusty plain with their lances held high, was invented by Chris to entertain his dinner party guests.

SERVES: 4
PREPARATION TIME: 20 minutes
COOKING TIME: 40 minutes
225g (8oz) red lentils, rinsed well
3 tablespoons groundnut oil
1 large onion, finely sliced
1 large green chilli, deseeded and finely chopped
1 large red chilli, deseeded and finely chopped
15g (½oz) fresh ginger, peeled and finely chopped
1 garlic clove, crushed
1 teaspoon ground turmeric
1 teaspoon ground coriander
1 teaspoon ground cumin
½ teaspoon freshly ground black pepper
275ml (½ pint) chicken stock (see page 9)
2 large tomatoes, chopped
100 ml (4 floz) coconut cream
1 dessertspoon salt
1 dessertspoon tamarind purée
15g (½oz) fresh coriander, chopped

TO GARNISH:
natural yoghurt

Put the lentils into a saucepan and pour in water to cover by 4cm. Bring to the boil and simmer fairly rapidly for 10 minutes, stirring from time to time and skimming any scum from the surface. Remove from the heat, cover tightly and set aside.

While the lentils are cooking, heat the oil and fry the onions over a moderate heat, stirring, for about 15-20 minutes until golden brown. Reduce the heat and stir in the green and red chillies, ginger and garlic. Cook gently, covered, for 3 minutes. Stir in the turmeric, coriander, cumin and black pepper and cook gently for 2 minutes, stirring. Add the stock, lentils, tomatoes, coconut cream, salt and tamarind purée and stir well. Increase the heat and bring almost, but not quite, to the boil. Cool a little, then blend in a 'liquidiser' until the soup is fairly, but not completely, smooth. Reheat the soup, stirring, until almost at boiling point. Remove from the heat and stir in the chopped coriander. Garnish with a spoonful of natural yoghurt and serve with warm naan bread.

Mulligatawny Soup

For the last few years we have worked with the National Trust, helping them to restore the gardens of the delightful 17th century Fenton House in Hampstead, London. An irrigation system, a vinehouse and terracotta borders have been constructed to bring the garden back to its former glory.

The National Trust also looks after Hughendon Manor in Buckinghamshire, the home of the great Victorian Prime Minister Benjamin Disraeli. This recipe, taken from Sara Paston-Williams' Art of Dining, published by the National Trust, was found in a notebook kept by Mary Anne Disraeli and discovered in her husband's study.

Malecotony or Mulligatawny Soup was a fashionable dish throughout the British Empire in the days of the Raj. Originating from southern India, the name is a derivative of the Tamil word 'milagutannir' meaning pepper-water. It appeared on smart menus of the time as 'soupe de L'Inde'. Judging by this mildly curried, but luscious and full-flavoured soup, Mary Anne Disraeli must have been a good cook!

SERVES: 6
PREPARATION AND COOKING TIME : 2 hours
75g (3oz) butter
1 small chicken
2 medium onions, finely chopped
1 tablespoon mild Madras curry powder
1 garlic clove, finely chopped
1 tablespoon plain flour
1.8 litres (3 pints) cold water
225g (8oz) lean ham, chopped in fine julienne
4 cloves
large pinch mace
sprig each of thyme, basil, marjoram
juice of 1 lemon
salt and freshly ground black pepper
1 tablespoon sour cream

Melt the butter in a large heavy-bottomed saucepan. Cut the chicken into pieces and brown all over. Remove from the pan and set aside. Sauté the onions until transparent and soft, then add the curry powder and garlic and cook for 2-3 minutes. Add the flour and cook for a further minute, stirring well. Gradually stir in the water and add the chicken. Add the ham, cloves, mace, herbs, lemon juice and seasoning, and bring to the boil. Turn down the heat and simmer for 1-1½ hours until the chicken is tender. Remove the chicken pieces from the pan with a slotted spoon. Strip all of the chicken meat and discard the skin and bones. Return the meat to the saucepan, remove the herbs and cloves and adjust the seasoning. Swirl in the sour cream just before serving.

Carrot & Cardamom Soup

(V) (F)

In 1988 we sold our first fresh soup, Carrot & Coriander. 11 years and 50 million carrots later it is still our best-selling recipe. Last year, to mark our 10th birthday, we produced this new sophisticated version with the seeds of cardamom pods used extensively in Arabia and India for their subtle flavour.

The inspiration came during a marketing department lunch at the newly opened Putney Bridge restaurant in London. Alison Adcock, following her tradition of eating soup every day of the year, was tempted by the Carrot & Cardamom on the menu. The combination was so delicious she rushed back to the factory, created the recipe for a lighter version, and the new soup was born.

SERVES: 4
PREPARATION AND COOKING TIME: 50 minutes

30g (1oz) butter
1 large onion, finely chopped
1 garlic clove, crushed
450g (1lb) (approx. 6) carrots, peeled and cut into equal size chunks
1 level tablespoon plain flour
850ml (1½ pints) vegetable stock (see page 14)
15g (½oz) creamed coconut
1 tablespoon lemon juice
seeds of 8 cardamom pods, crushed with a pestle & mortar
1 teaspoon sugar
salt and freshly ground black pepper

TO GARNISH:

toasted coconut shavings
cook fresh coconut shavings quickly in a dry pan

Melt the butter and cook the onion, garlic and carrots gently in a large covered saucepan for 5 minutes, without colouring. Add the flour and cook gently for 2 minutes. Stir in the stock, creamed coconut and lemon juice. Cover, bring to the boil and simmer gently for about 15 minutes until the carrots are tender. Cool a little, then purée in a liquidiser until smooth. Add the cardamom and sugar and season to taste. Reheat gently and serve with a twist of black pepper or chill and serve ice-cold. Garnish with toasted coconut shavings.

Cau Lau

(V) (F)

Travelling is part of Vanessa Bellamy's life, either for work setting up and running international press offices for major events like the Louis Vuitton America's Cup Challengers Trophy or for pleasure. When she travelled extensively through Vietnam she found it to be a wonderful country full of remarkable people. The food varied from familiar stir fries to noodle soups, and from rice flour pancakes to dog kebabs.

Not being a meat-eater, this is Vanessa's vegetarian interpretation of a noodle-based soup that impressed her in the magic town of Hoi An. She has used smoked tofu to replace the pork. It's a local speciality because the noodles, made with the town's spring water, are exclusive to Hoi An. Fortunately, you can now buy good alternatives over here.

In Vietnam, fish sauce is generally used as a dipping sauce for spring rolls, but Vanessa loves it so much that she uses it to make this dressing, given to her by a Vietnamese girlfriend, to accompany the Cau Lau. The sauce and garnish are essential for the contrast in flavours and textures. Use generous amounts of them.

SERVES: 4
PREPARATION AND COOKING TIME: 40 minutes
8 tablespoons groundnut oil
2 small onions, finely chopped
4 sticks lemon grass, outer leaves removed and finely chopped
5cm (2") piece fresh ginger, peeled and finely chopped
4 cloves garlic, peeled and finely chopped
1.2 litres (2 pints) vegetable stock (see page 14)
8 fresh lime leaves
225g (8oz) smoked tofu, cubed
2 packets fresh Shanghai noodles

TO GARNISH
baby spinach leaves, coriander leaves, mint leaves, torn
bean sprouts
cucumber julienne
carrot julienne
roasted raw peanuts

FOR THE SOUP DRESSING:
2 tablespoons nam pla, Thai fish sauce
4 tablespoons water
2 tablespoons sweet chilli sauce
juice of ½-1 lemon
2 garlic cloves, peeled and cut into slivers
sugar to taste

Put the oil into a saucepan and heat gently. Add the onion, lemon grass, ginger and garlic and cook for 2 minutes, without colouring. Add the vegetable stock and lime leaves, and simmer for 20 minutes to allow all of the flavours to infuse. Then add the smoked tofu and simmer for 5 minutes more.

Meanwhile, soak the noodles in boiling water for 5 minutes, then drain and divide into 4 soup bowls. Ladle the broth into the bowls then top with the garnish ingredients. Combine the dressing ingredients in a bowl and whisk well together. Serve as an accompaniment to the soup.

Thai Spinach Soup

(V) (F)

Because it has such a pronounced flavour, people tend to love or hate spinach. We adore it. We also think it is very underrated as far as soup-making is concerned. We have produced many different spinach soups, all of which have had a huge following. So for those of you who share our weakness, here is one of our bestsellers.

TIP: Most children hate spinach soup; most children love 'green' soup. Bear that in mind! The exception is our Managing Director's son - he loves spinach soup!

SERVES: 4
PREPARATION TIME: 15 minutes
COOKING TIME: 30 minutes
25g (1oz) butter
1 medium onion, finely chopped
1 medium potato, about 225g (8oz), roughly chopped
1 garlic clove, crushed
1 teaspoon ground cumin
1 litre (1¾ pints) vegetable stock (see page 14)
50g (2oz) creamed coconut
250g (9oz) fresh spinach
salt and freshly ground black pepper
2 tablespoons fresh coriander, chopped
lemon or lime juice to taste

TO GARNISH:
crème fraîche
crispy onions (see page 142)

Melt the butter and cook the onion, potato and garlic in a covered saucepan for 10 minutes, without colouring. Stir in the cumin and cook for 2 minutes. Add the vegetable stock. Cover, bring to the boil and simmer gently for 15 minutes. Stir in the creamed coconut and spinach, cool a little, allowing the spinach to wilt, then purée in a liquidiser until smooth. Taste for seasoning. Reheat gently and stir in the coriander and lemon or lime juice to taste. Serve with swirls of crème fraîche and a sprinkling of crispy onions.

Far East Hot Pepper & Turkey Soup

"Something that conjures up warm sunshine and far away places, when you're looking at grey skies" is how Susan Riddy describes her exotic creation that won 2nd prize in our 1998 'Create a Soup' competition.
Susan draws upon the influences of the many countries she has visited during her travels, where sharing meals and learning new dishes have inspired her creativity in cooking.
Susan's recipe is not just a way to use up Christmas turkey leftovers, but a sensational spicy broth with slivers of red and yellow peppers, beansprouts and chunks of turkey.
Susan prefers hers with star anise dumplings rather than bread (see page 144 for the recipe). A multicoloured and exotic meal in a bowl.

SERVES: 4
PREPARATION AND COOKING TIME: 1 hour

3 tablespoons olive oil (preferably infused with a sprig of fresh rosemary)
1 small red onion, finely sliced
25g (1oz) (approx 1") fresh root ginger, peeled and finely sliced
1 red pepper, finely sliced
1 yellow pepper, finely sliced
3 garlic cloves, crushed
500g (1lb 2oz) (approx. 4) turkey breasts, cut into 1½" dice
2 teaspoons Chinese five spice seasoning
2-3 teaspoons thick, hot chilli sauce
2 teaspoons garam masala
2 teaspoons tomato paste
250g (9oz) fresh beansprouts
225ml (8floz) chicken stock (see page 9)
2 teaspoons cornflour
100ml (4floz) mango juice
approx. 2 teaspoons salt
1 bunch fresh coriander
zest of 1 lime

Heat the oil in a large covered saucepan or wok, and fry the red onion, ginger and red and yellow peppers gently for 5 minutes, without colouring. Turn the heat down, add the garlic and continue to cook very gently for 5 minutes. Move the vegetables to one side and add the diced turkey to the bottom of the pan. Turn up the heat and stir the meat quickly to brown, adding a little more oil if necessary. Stir in the Chinese five spice seasoning, chilli sauce, garam masala, tomato paste and half the beansprouts, cover and cook very gently for 5 minutes, stirring from time to time.
Add a third of the stock and mix well.
Mix the cornflour to a smooth paste with a little stock and stir into the soup with the remaining stock and mango juice. Taste for seasoning, adding salt as required. Bring to the boil and simmer gently for 5 minutes or until the turkey is cooked. Sit the rest of the beansprouts on top of the soup along with a handful of roughly torn coriander leaves and the lime zest. Cover, remove from the heat and allow to rest for 5 minutes to infuse the lime and coriander.
Serve in deep Chinese bowls.

Thai Hot & Sour Mushroom Soup (V) (F)

The many delights of Thai food have found their way into British kitchens over the last decade. We wanted to make a clear hot and sour broth using the 5 main authentic Thai flavour combinations - salty, sour, sweet, spicy and herby - and this was the result. When we produced our cartoned version it also turned out to be ideal for dieters, with a mere 7 calories per 100ml!

Most Asians love chillies and because they radiate inner warmth, they give a sense of wellbeing when eaten. Some Thai and Indonesian dishes, such as 'ayam rica-rica', contain up to 40 chillies! You may be relieved to know our soup doesn't, but be warned, it is still pretty hot. Enjoy a bowl on its own or add some glass noodles to turn it into a meal in itself.

TIP: Wash your hands well after preparing chillies to avoid any nasty burning sensations to your fingers, eyes, nose and lips.

SERVES: 4
PREPARATION AND COOKING TIME: 45 minutes
850 ml (1½ pints) vegetable stock (see page 14)
1 lemongrass, bruised
5 kaffir lime leaves, roughly torn
2 tablespoons light soy sauce
1 teaspoon sugar
2 tablespoons lemon juice
250g (9oz) oyster mushrooms, roughly separated
1 carrot, peeled and cut into fine matchsticks
1 or 2 red or green chillies, seeded and roughly sliced

FOR THE NAM PRIK POW SAUCE:
4 tablespoons sunflower oil
3 garlic cloves, finely chopped
3 shallots, finely chopped
2 large red chillies, seeded and roughly chopped
150 ml (¼ pint) water
2 tablespoons sugar
1 teaspoon salt

TO GARNISH:
2 tablespoons fresh coriander leaves
110g (4oz) bean sprouts

To make the nam prik pow sauce, heat the oil and fry the garlic over a moderate heat until golden brown. Remove and set aside. In the same pan, fry the shallots until crisp and golden. Remove and set aside. In the same pan, fry the chillies until darkened. Remove and purée in a liquidiser with the garlic, shallots and water until smooth. In the same pan, reheat the oil and add the paste, sugar and salt. Mix well and cook until the paste becomes dark, reddish brown.

To make the soup, pour the vegetable stock into a large saucepan and add the nam prik pow sauce and the rest of the ingredients. Cover, bring to the boil and simmer gently for about 10 minutes until the mushrooms are tender but firm. Serve garnished with coriander leaves and bean sprouts.

Gingered Prawns & Citrus Vegetable Julienne

Poet and school cook Yvonne Campbell is always playing about with new recipe ideas and experimenting with different combinations of ingredients. In the spirit of true invention, most of her recipes are arrived at by trial and error and the results inflicted upon her husband. This pretty pale pink soup of prawns and vegetables is the result of such an occasion. Quite a complicated, and at times fiddly recipe to make, the result is truly inspirational. The chicken livers are a surprising addition, but the combination works.

SERVES: 4
PREPARATION AND COOKING TIME: 3½ hours
Pre-heat the oven to 200°C/400°F/Gas Mark 6

FOR THE STOCK:
225g (8oz) chicken livers, washed and drained well
2 chicken thighs, skinned
570ml (1 pint) water
1 small onion, roughly chopped

1 small carrot, peeled
1 small parsnip, peeled
1 small potato, peeled
salt and freshly ground black pepper

FOR THE SOUP:
6 tomatoes, skinned and roughly chopped
1 teaspoon Worcestershire sauce
1 teaspoon Dijon mustard
570ml (1 pint) stock (see above)
25g (1oz) medium oatmeal
juice of ½ orange
juice of ½ lemon
15g (½oz) freshly grated root ginger
275ml (½ pint) water
flesh of ½ grapefruit, all pith and skin removed, cut into small pieces.
225g (8oz) prawns, peeled and cooked
1 egg yolk, beaten
salt and freshly ground black pepper

To make the stock, put all the stock ingredients into a medium saucepan. Cover, bring to the boil and simmer gently for 1 hour. Gently remove the carrot, parsnip and potato, keeping them whole. Pass the liquid through a fine sieve into a clean bowl and reserve.

To make the soup, put the tomatoes into a saucepan with the Worcestershire sauce and the mustard. Cook gently for 10 minutes to break up the tomatoes. Bring the stock to the boil and stir in the oatmeal. Add this to the tomato mixture. Simmer gently for 30 minutes until the mixture is thickish but not gloopy.

Meanwhile, prepare the vegetables from the stock. Cut them into matchsticks. Put the carrots and potatoes in a small baking dish and pour over the orange juice. Put the parsnips into a small baking dish and pour over the lemon juice. Bake both dishes in the oven for 30 minutes.

Put the ginger into a small saucepan with the water. Bring to the boil, then simmer gently for 10 minutes. Cool. Add the grapefruit pieces and the prawns and leave to marinate for 30 minutes.

When the tomato mixture is ready, remove from the heat and stir in the well-beaten yolk. Pass through a fine sieve. Add the baked matchstick vegetables and gingered grapefruit and prawns, then season to taste. Reheat and serve.

Papaya & Ginger Gazpacho with Shitake Mushrooms

(V) (F)

Every time Shirley Posner creates an interesting new soup recipe, she sends it to Alison, our New Product Development Manager. Shirley, a true food enthusiast, first struck up a friendship with Alison whilst studying Food & Consumer Studies at University.

Shirley now lives in Singapore and created the recipe for BEAM, the magazine for the British Association of Singapore. Papayas are virtually fat free and packed with vitamins, and can now be found at most major supermarkets. Its worth tracking down all the ingredients, and the hot garnish makes this chilled soup the height of sophistication.

SERVES: 4
PREPARATION AND COOKING TIME: 30 minutes

2 tablespoons sunflower oil
2 large onions, finely sliced
4 garlic cloves, crushed
110g (4oz) (approx 4-5") fresh root ginger, peeled and finely sliced
2 large papayas (paw paw)
500ml (17½ floz) mango and orange juice
Juice of 2 large limes
Salt and freshly ground black pepper

TO GARNISH:

2 tablespoons sunflower oil
2 garlic cloves, crushed
225g (8oz) Shitake mushrooms
2 tablespoons single cream
4 spring onions, finely sliced diagonally

Heat the oil and cook the onion, garlic and ginger gently in a large covered saucepan for 10 minutes, without colouring. Leave to cool. Meanwhile, cut the papaya in half lengthways. Discard the seeds and scoop out the flesh. Place the papaya, onion mixture, mango and orange juice and lime juice in a liquidiser and purée until very smooth. Taste for seasoning and chill well.

When ready to serve, prepare the garnish. Heat the oil and cook the garlic gently for 2 minutes without colouring. Add the mushrooms and fry over a moderate heat for 5 minutes, stirring. Taste for seasoning, then, while piping hot, spoon into the centre of each bowl of chilled soup. Drizzle cream over the mushrooms, sprinkle with spring onions and serve.

Chinese Leaves & Pepper Soup

From her home in Dunbartonshire, Fenella Taylor liaises with the Scottish media for us. As her family has steadily increased, we have never ceased to be amazed at her continued energy and enthusiasm. This recipe of Fenella's great-aunt Miriam was cooked by members of her family frequently when Fenella was young - it was then included in a cookery book her mother compiled for her and her 3 siblings so they wouldn't go hungry when they left home. Fenella describes it as "her bible". This fabulously rich and fluffy soup is a perfect way to use up these 'poor relation' vegetables that are left at the bottom of organic vegetable deliveries. The pleasant surprise is that you don't have to be a great fan of either vegetable to love this soup.

SERVES: 6
PREPARATION AND COOKING TIME: 40 minutes
2 tablespoons extra virgin olive oil
50g (2oz) butter
225g (8oz) green peppers, deseeded and finely diced
2 medium onions, finely chopped
½ head of Chinese leaves, finely shredded
2 tablespoons plain flour
425ml (3/4 pint) chicken stock (see page 9)
425ml (3/4 pint) milk
3 tablespoons single cream
salt and freshly ground black pepper to taste

Heat oil in a saucepan, add the butter and melt. Add the green pepper, onion and Chinese leaves and cook for 5 minutes. Stir in the flour and cook for 1 more minute. Add the stock and bring to the boil, then turn down the heat and simmer until the vegetables are cooked. Add the milk, cool then blend until smooth in a liquidiser. Return to the saucepan then add the cream. Taste for seasoning.

Black Bean & Carrot Soup (V)(F)

Talented photographer, Patrick Boyd, made it to the final of one of our soup creating competitions with this excellent recipe, dreamt up whilst living in Japan. Patrick and his wife Susan missed a variety of pulses as they could only buy soya beans or very expensive kidney beans. When Patrick was sent off to a conference in San José, he brought back two sacks of black beans. His next problem was what to do with them! Thus a soup was born.

Since the competition, not only has Patrick done some super photography for us, but he often plays football with Simon Bell, our Managing Director.

SERVES: 6-8
PREPARATION AND COOKING TIME:
overnight soak plus 1 hour 55 minutes

250g (9oz) dried black beans, soaked overnight
110g (4oz) butter
2 onions, coarsely chopped
5 cloves garlic, coarsely chopped
6 bay leaves
500g (1lb 2oz) carrots, coarsely chopped
25ml (1floz) Jalapeño Tabasco sauce or
        1 tablespoon of chopped Jalapeño chillies
150ml (¼ pint) sherry or fortified wine
75g (3oz) tomato purée
salt and freshly ground black pepper   TO GARNISH:
1·2 litres (2 pints) water   Cheddar cheese, grated

Boil the soaked black beans in water rapidly for about 15 minutes. Then simmer while the rest of the soup is prepared. Melt the butter and sauté the onions, garlic and bay leaves in a large saucepan until the onions are soft. Add the carrots and Jalapeño sauce or chillies. Cover and sweat the carrots for 5 minutes. Pour in the sherry and simmer for another 15 minutes. Add the drained black beans, tomato purée, seasoning and cover with 2 pints of water. Bring to the boil and then simmer for 1 hour. Remove from the heat, remove the bay leaves and purée in a liquidiser. Reheat. Season to taste and serve garnished with grated cheddar cheese.

Cream of Carrot & Kiwi Soup with Orange Peppers

Besides running a butterfly farm in Sherborne, Dorset, Rosemary and Robert Goodden have set up Worldlife, a conservation charity. Their butterfly farm, open to the public from April to October, supplied the silk for the wedding dress of Diana, Princess of Wales. It is the only silk farm in the country.

With three children adding to the workload, it is amazing that Rosemary has had any spare time to create such an original recipe using this unusual combination of ingredients. She first became interested in soup whilst cooking up simple recipes to raise funds for Christian Aid. While this recipe is easy to make, its flavours are both complex and sophisticated. It is also very attractive. The Gooddens prefer theirs piping hot, but we think it is delicious chilled.

SERVES : 4
PREPARATION AND COOKING TIME : 40 minutes
50g (2oz) butter
1 medium onion, roughly chopped
1 large garlic clove, crushed
1 large orange pepper, finely chopped
450g (1lb) carrots, roughly chopped
725ml (1¼ pints) chicken stock (see page 9)
290ml (½ pint) milk
½ teaspoon sugar
2 sprigs of fresh rosemary, finely chopped
salt and freshly ground black pepper
4 kiwi fruit, peeled, quartered and sliced very thinly

Melt the butter and cook the onions and garlic gently for 5 minutes in a covered saucepan, without colouring. Add ¾ of the orange pepper and cook for 1 minute. Stir in the carrots and stock. Cover the saucepan, bring to the boil and simmer gently for 15 minutes until the vegetables are tender. Add the milk. Cool a little, then purée in a liquidiser until smooth. Return to the saucepan and add the remaining orange pepper, sugar, rosemary and taste for seasoning. Reheat gently and cook for 10 minutes, stirring from time to time. Add the kiwi fruit and warm through. Serve piping hot, or chilled, with a grind of black pepper on top.

Spicy Sweet Potato
& Butternut Soup

This recipe travelled halfway round the world before it won our 1997 'Create a Soup' competition, run through the BBC Good Food magazine.

Georgina Vance, then a paediatric anaesthetist at St. George's Hospital in London, tried a similar soup in a delicatessen in Perth, Australia. When she returned to London with her antipodean husband, she missed it so much that she set about trying to copy it. She found sweet potatoes for sale near work in Tooting and played around with the ingredients until she perfected the recipe.

At the end of 1997, Georgina and her husband emigrated to Australia. Luckily for us, she left the recipe!

SERVES: 4
PREPARATION AND COOKING TIME: 35 minutes
1 tablespoon light olive oil
1 medium onion, finely chopped
2 garlic cloves, crushed
1 teaspoon cumin seeds, roasted lightly and ground
1 teaspoon coriander seeds, roasted lightly and ground
2 tablespoons sesame seeds, roasted lightly
1cm (½") fresh root ginger, peeled and finely grated
1 green chilli, seeded and chopped, or to taste
zest and juice of 1 lime
1 teaspoon runny honey
340g (12oz) sweet potato, peeled and cut into 2.5cm (1") dice
340g (12oz) butternut squash, peeled and cut into 2.5cm (1") dice
1.2 litres (2 pints) vegetable stock (see page 14)
1 x 400g (14oz) tin of chickpeas, drained
salt and freshly ground black pepper
handful of fresh coriander leaves, chopped

TO GARNISH:
150ml (¼ pint) natural yoghurt or
Sweet Red Pepper Butter (see page 141)

Heat the oil and cook the onion and garlic in a covered saucepan for 10 minutes, without colouring. Stir in the spices, sesame seeds, ginger, chilli, lime zest and honey and stir for 30 seconds. Add the sweet potato, butternut squash, juice of half a lime and the stock. Cover, bring to the boil and simmer for about 10 minutes, or until the vegetables are almost tender. Add the chickpeas and taste for seasoning. Simmer for 10 minutes, then add the remaining lime juice to taste. Cool a little, then purée in a liquidiser until very smooth, adding more stock if necessary to achieve the required consistency. Reheat gently and stir in the coriander just before serving. Serve with a swirl of natural yoghurt or float a disc of Sweet Red Pepper butter on top.

Coconut Corn Soup

Ⓥ Ⓕ

Food writer, stylist and self-confessed cookbookaholic Antonia Locke was one of the finalists in our 1998 'Create a Soup' competition, run through the Daily Telegraph, with this fabulous recipe. We then asked her to help us with recipe-testing for this book. Antonia likes to combine her passion for travelling with learning different styles of cooking and discovering new ingredients. After travelling to Australia, where she immersed herself in the best of Pacific Rim cuisine, she wanted to create a soup that would reflect this trend of fusion cooking. It is a joy to look at - bright yellow with flecks of red pepper and green coriander. The flavour is not too spicy, very delicate, and ever so slightly sweet. Shredded chicken or noodles can be added to make it more substantial.

SERVES: 4
PREPARATION AND COOKING TIME: 50 minutes
2 tablespoons vegetable oil
3 medium onions, finely sliced
2 garlic cloves, crushed
1-2 tablespoons root ginger, peeled and freshly grated
1½ teaspoons turmeric
425ml (¾ pint) coconut milk
1 litre (1¾ pints) vegetable stock (see page 14)
340g (12oz) sweetcorn kernels, preferably fresh
1 red pepper, seeded and finely diced
1 lemongrass, bruised
3 tablespoons fresh coriander leaves, chopped
2 tablespoons Thai fish sauce
2 tablespoons maple syrup
lime juice to taste

TO GARNISH:
2 tablespoons fresh coriander leaves, chopped

Heat the oil and cook the onions over a moderate heat for about 15 minutes until soft and lightly browned. If they begin to stick, add a few drops of water. Lower the heat, stir in the garlic, ginger and turmeric and cook for 1 minute. Add the coconut milk, vegetable stock, sweetcorn, red pepper and lemongrass. Cover, bring to the boil and simmer gently for 10 minutes until the corn is tender. Remove from the heat and discard the lemongrass. Add the coriander.

Mix the fish sauce, maple syrup and lime juice together in a bowl, then add a little to the soup and taste, continuing to add little by little until a balanced taste is achieved. Serve garnished with fresh coriander leaves.

Mango Soup

Alison Clay invented this incredibly simple summer soup during a year's sojourn in the French West Indies. It proved to be a great success at her parties, and, having tried it, we can see why. She sent us the recipe 3 years ago, but when we tried to track her down, the trail went cold in Saudi Arabia. We hope she is still throwing parties and delighting her guests with cool spoonfuls of this irresistible mango soup.

SERVES: 4
PREPARATION AND COOKING TIME: 20 minutes
3 large ripe mangoes, peeled and flesh removed to a bowl
freshly grated zest of ½ orange
juice of 1 orange
1 teaspoon fresh root ginger, grated
250ml (9floz) natural yoghurt
500ml (17½ floz) milk
salt to taste
1 dessertspoon balsamic vinegar

TO GARNISH:
1 dessertspoon yoghurt
2 tablespoons fresh coriander leaves, chopped

Put the mango pulp, orange zest and juice, and ginger into a liquidiser and purée until very smooth. Pass through a fine sieve into a clean bowl and stir in the yoghurt, milk, salt to taste and balsamic vinegar. Cover and chill well. Serve with a dessertspoon of yoghurt and sprinkled with chopped fresh coriander leaves.

Cariberry Soup

Clare Lillywhite had an exotic childhood. Though British, she was born in the Sudan, then moved to the West Indies at the age of 8, where she became familiar with local dishes. Now living in Northumberland, Clare is still keen on cooking. She makes cheese and yoghurt and, until recently, kept her own hens. Her soup is an old family recipe, which combines garden redcurrants with typically Jamaican ingredients, reflecting British and West Indian experiences. Clare suggests eating this soup before any kind of game, although in Jamaica it teams up perfectly with a good goat curry!

SERVES: 4
PREPARATION AND COOKING TIME: 55 minutes
25 g (1oz) butter
1 tablespoon sunflower oil
675 g (1½ lb) onions, finely sliced
2 medium sweet potatoes, about 500 g (1lb 2oz), diced
900 g (2lb) redcurrants, stalks removed, reserving 4 sprigs
            of currants on their stalks for the garnish
850 ml (1½ pints) chicken stock (see page 9)
1½ teaspoons curry powder
6 juniper berries
275 ml (½ pint) coconut milk
salt and freshly ground black pepper

(optional - honey/maple syrup to taste)

TO GARNISH:
sprinkling of icing sugar

Melt the butter and oil and cook the onions over a moderate heat until golden, stirring. Add the sweet potatoes, redcurrants, stock, curry powder and juniper berries. Cover, bring to the boil and simmer gently until soft. Cool a little, then purée in a liquidiser. Return to a gentle heat. Add coconut milk to taste and, if necessary, a little water to thin the soup. Taste for seasoning and for sweetness, adding honey or maple syrup if desired. Pass the soup through a fine sieve. Season to taste and serve chilled, garnished with the remaining berry sprigs and a sprinkling of icing sugar.

Curried Banana Soup

A friend of a friend, Fiona Carson, gave us this unusual thick soup that she and her husband David ate whilst at their luxurious honeymoon hideaway hotel on Antigua. Every night they sat down to six courses on a verandah overlooking a fragrant tropical garden. The recipe for this memorable soup was on a menu card that Fiona saved as a memento. A rather bizarre soup, it is actually surprisingly good. Thickened with rice and mildly curried, the flavour is reminiscent of baked bananas - eat as part of a Caribbean meal, perhaps followed by barbecued fish.

SERVES: 6
PREPARATION AND COOKING TIME: 35 minutes
50g (2oz) butter
1 clove garlic, finely chopped
1 medium onion, peeled and finely chopped
1 tablespoon mild Madras curry powder
110g (4oz) Basmati rice
1.25 litres (2¼ pints) chicken stock (see page 9)
250ml (9 floz) single cream
2 ripe bananas, peeled and cut into chunks
juice of ½ a lime
salt and freshly ground pepper to taste

TO GARNISH:
sweet potato crisps

Melt the butter in a saucepan, add the garlic and onion and sauté until transparent and soft. Add the curry powder and cook for a further 2 to 3 minutes. Add the rice and chicken stock, bring to the boil, then turn down the heat and simmer for approximately 25 minutes, until the rice is soft. Cool and pour into a liquidiser, add the single cream and bananas and process until smooth. Return to the pan and add the lime juice. Taste for seasoning and garnish with sweet potato crisps.

Ceviche

Joel Langford and his brother Adam are the third generation of Langfords to run their antique silver business from the London Silver Vaults. When not dealing in silverware and writing books on the subject, Joel Langford loves to cook and is a real perfectionist in the kitchen.

Joel's first honeymoon to Mexico in the '70s - when, unusually, he was accompanied by not only his American bride but also one of his best male friends - triggered his keen interest in replicating authentic Mexican recipes.

Popular throughout Latin America, Ceviche literally translated means 'dry soup' and relies on the juice of fresh limes to pickle the raw fish and to provide a little liquid. However, we love this refreshing recipe with the addition of a dash of vinegar and iced water. We leave it to you to decide whether you prefer it wet or dry.

SERVES: 4

PREPARATION AND COOKING TIME : Overnight plus 20 minutes

900g (2lb) firm white fish, eg seabass, red mullet, cod, haddock, salmon, skinned and cut into 1cm (1") cubes
juice of 8 limes
2 garlic cloves, crushed
4 tablespoons red wine vinegar
4 tablespoons fruity extra virgin olive oil
290ml (½ pint) iced water
1 large red onion, finely sliced
1 bunch of spring onions, white part only, finely sliced
4 large ripe tomatoes, peeled and chopped into ½ cm (¼") pieces
1 yellow pepper, seeded and finely chopped
2-3 large red chillies, halved, seeded and finely sliced
3 tablespoons fresh coriander leaves, chopped
Salt

TO GARNISH:
1 quantity fresh, hot garlic croûtons (see page 142)

Put the fish into a bowl and pour in the lime juice to cover the fish. Stir to ensure each fish cube is coated in lime juice and marinate for 4 hours or, if possible, overnight in the refrigerator. Purée the garlic, red wine vinegar and olive oil in a liquidiser. Pour into a bowl, stir in the water and toss with the red onion, spring onions, tomatoes yellow pepper, chillies and 1 tablespoon of chopped coriander leaves and marinate for 4 hours or if possible, overnight in the refrigerator.

When ready to serve, toss all the ingredients together, including the remaining coriander leaves and taste for seasoning. Serve in wide bowls and offer hot croûtons to your guests.

Tortilla Soup

Sofia Craxton, one of our recipe development team, is Mexican and met her English husband at a 1986 World Cup football match in Mexico City. He persuaded her to come to England but, as a lover of food and a graduate of food science, she's never forgotten the shock of having to acclimatise herself to our cuisine! Now, with the plethora of international ingredients available, she doesn't find it as bad, and we have gained from her immense, in-depth knowledge of chillies and spices. This, according to Sofia, is 'the most Mexican of soups'; it is served on special occasions and is claimed to be good for a hangover!

SERVES: 6
PREPARATION AND COOKING TIME: 40 minutes

1 tablespoon groundnut oil
1 medium onion, finely chopped
2 cloves garlic, finely chopped
4 ripe tomatoes, roughly chopped
1 dried ancho chilli, de-seeded
1.35 litres (2¼ pints) chicken stock (see page 9)
30 yellow or white corn tortilla chips
2 avocados, peeled, pitted and sliced
110g (4oz) feta cheese
110g (4oz) crème fraîche
fresh coriander leaves, chopped
4 limes, halved

Soak the chilli in 150ml (¼ pint) boiling water for 5 minutes, or until soft. Add the soaking water to the stock and finely chop the chilli.

Heat the oil in a saucepan, then add the onion, garlic, chopped tomatoes and chilli. Sauté for 5 minutes. Put the mixture into a liquidiser, add 2 tablespoons of stock and process until smooth. Return to the pan and add the remainder of the stock, bring to the boil, then turn down the heat and simmer for about 20 minutes. Add the tortilla chips and simmer until they become soft. Serve garnished with avocado, feta cheese, crème fraîche, coriander leaves and a squeeze of lime juice. Cut the remaining 3 limes in ½ and serve with each bowl.

Cajun & Ginger Gumbo

Sara Holman-Howes and her husband Keith knew they had found something special when they took over the freehold of the Earle Arms in the beautiful, isolated village of Heydon in Norfolk. Made up of many small rooms, it is traditional and intimate. Sara and Keith have worked hard to develop it from 'a hell-hole with a condemned kitchen' to a thriving business serving brilliant food.

Sara's cooking style reflects her childhood in the multicultural atmosphere of Toronto, where she was exposed to the cuisines of 'every nation under the sun'.

To this hot, rich and almost sauce-like base with just a hint of peanut, Sara adds typically Cajun ingredients to create a richly flavoured meal in a bowl.

Unbeknown to each other at the time, both Sara and Keith entered our 1998 'Create a Soup' competition. As Keith is the more serious cook of the two, Sara has been wondering how to tell him that her recipe has been chosen for this book rather than his. Well now he'll know!

TIP: In Cajun cookery, gumbos are usually spooned onto a bowl of rice.

SERVES: 4
PREPARATION AND COOKING TIME: 40 minutes

3 tablespoons olive oil
1 small onion, finely chopped
2 large garlic cloves, crushed
50g (2oz) fresh root ginger, finely grated
1 medium red chilli, finely chopped (with seeds)
½ teaspoon salt
½ teaspoon freshly ground black pepper
50g (2oz) butter
50g (2oz) plain flour
400ml (14 fl oz) milk
400ml (14 fl oz) fresh unsweetened orange juice
Juice and zest of 1 orange
2 teaspoons Dijon mustard
1 level teaspoon peanut butter
2 tablespoons soy sauce
2 tablespoons fresh chives, snipped
2 tablespoons fresh flat leaf parsley, chopped
salt and freshly ground black pepper

TO COMPLETE THE GUMBO, CHOOSE FROM ONE OF THE FOLLOWING:

2 chargrilled chicken breasts
or 2 thick slices boiled bacon and black beans
or 2 225g (8oz) roasted salmon steaks
250g (9oz) cooked patty pan, quartered
1 tablespoon of peanut butter
2 tablespoons fresh chives, snipped
2 tablespoons fresh flat leaf parsley, chopped

Heat the oil and cook the onion, garlic, ginger, chilli, salt and pepper for 1 minute, stirring. Add the butter and flour, and cook very gently until the mixture has a nutty colour and aroma. Take off the heat and gradually whisk in the milk. Return to the heat and bring to the boil. Add the orange juice and zest, mustard, peanut butter, soy sauce, chives and parsley. Taste for seasoning and simmer gently for 5 minutes. Serve hot with one of the suggestions.

Spicy Corn Chowder Ⓥ Ⓕ

Chowder comes from the French word 'chaudière' meaning a fish kettle. This style of soup is very popular all over the USA, which is where Sofia Craxton, one of our recipe developers, gained inspiration. She spent 2 months at our factory in San Francisco, and saw how successfully Californians combine their wonderful seasonal ingredients with the numerous ethnic influences of the region. Sofia created this pretty, creamy soup with sweetcorn and an interesting mix of jalapeño and ancho chillies. Coming from Mexico, she is our resident chilli expert! Serve with warm tortillas or corn and chilli muffins (see page 134).

SERVES: 4
PREPARATION AND COOKING TIME: 1 hour
2 tablespoons extra virgin olive oil
1 medium onion, finely chopped
1 garlic clove, crushed
2 sticks celery, finely chopped
1 large carrot, very finely chopped
225g (8oz) potato, peeled and ½ roughly, ½ finely chopped
1 x 340g (12oz) tin sweetcorn, drained
½ teaspoon powdered ancho chilli
725ml (1¼ pints) water
1 small red pepper, seeded and finely chopped
½ medium green pepper, seeded and finely chopped
1 level teaspoon bottled jalapeño peppers
75ml (3floz) double cream
salt

TO GARNISH:
fresh tomato or citrus fruit salsa
2 tablespoons fresh coriander leaves, chopped

Heat the oil and cook the onion over a moderate heat for about 15 minutes until golden. Add the garlic and cook for 1 minute, then add the celery, ½ of the carrot, the roughly chopped potato, ½ of the sweetcorn and the ancho chilli and cook gently for 2 minutes. Add the water, cover, bring to the boil and simmer gently for about 15 minutes until the vegetables are tender. Cool a little, then purée in a liquidiser until very smooth. Return to a clean saucepan and stir in the red, green and jalapeño peppers and the remaining carrot, finely chopped potato and sweetcorn. Cover, bring to the boil and simmer gently for 10 minutes. Stir in the double cream. Taste for seasoning and reheat gently. Serve garnished with fresh tomato or citrus fruit salsa and chopped fresh coriander leaves.

Citrus Berry Soup ⓥ

As big fans of sweet soups, we wanted to include this lovely, tangy offering as an example of a real pudding soup. Imagine an unfrozen dusky pink, home-made ice-cream with a gorgeous creamy texture and a slightly tart taste. Garnish with blueberries and a sprinkling of icing sugar and give your tastebuds an adventure not to be missed!

SERVES: 4
PREPARATION AND COOKING TIME: 15 minutes

500g (1lb 2oz) blueberries
425ml (3/4 pint) plain low fat yoghurt
290ml (1/2 pint) fresh orange juice
4 tablespoons light crème fraîche
2 tablespoons grated lemon zest
        (approx. 4 lemons)
1 teaspoon ground cinnamon

TO GARNISH:
4 dessertspoons Greek yoghurt
4 teaspoons runny honey
or
whole blueberries
icing sugar for sprinkling

Purée all the ingredients in a liquidiser until smooth. Pass through a fine sieve. Chill well. Serve with a spoonful of Greek yoghurt and drizzle with honey or a few blueberries and a sprinkling of icing sugar.

Beans

Beans

Beans are probably one of the most versatile varieties of vegetable used in cooking. Whilst the classic green bean falls into the group of those with edible pods, the varieties of beans where only the seeds can be eaten is huge.

The wonderful thing about any type of pulse is they act as sponges, soaking up the flavours and nuances of the dish in which they are cooked. They can be combined with other ingredients in almost limitless ways, including soups, stews, casseroles and salads. They happily jump from one culture to another, adapting to the particular character of each country and its cooking.

Beans, peas and lentils can be cooked from fresh or dried, depending on the variety. Dried tend to be more common, unless you have a wonderful fresh supply in your garden or a good greengrocer. The quality of tinned pulses is getting better, and they are certainly much more convenient than dried, but the taste and texture of pulses cooked from scratch usually compensates for the preparation time.

As well as their versatility, excellent flavours and ability to add texture and substance, beans and grains are also naturally low in fat, and packed with protein, vitamins and minerals.

We have in fact also thrown in a few grains recipes, not only because of their affinity to pulses, but also because they share with beans the wonderful ability to absorb and carry flavour.

If relatively new to cooking with dried beans, you may find the following useful:

- Use the freshest beans you can find. When old they take longer to cook, will not be as tender and crumble if overcooked

- Don't forget to pick through them carefully before cooking, and rinse well to get rid of dirt and dust

- Beans that have been properly soaked and cooked can be frozen, just thaw before reheating

- Some varieties can be boiled rapidly for an hour or so instead of an overnight soak. But remember, any type of dried pulse must always be re-hydrated and cooked properly. Always check the specific instructions for the variety you are using and don't skimp on the recommended time

- Generally, the longer the beans are soaked, the shorter the cooking time and the more tender the result

- Cooking beans with salt or acidic ingredients such as tomatoes, lemon or wine will toughen the skins and lengthen the cooking time. Try to add salt towards the end, once they are tender

Fresh Baked Beans

(V)

This is the story of how we came about the idea of putting fresh beans into cartons, so if you're sitting comfortably, we'll begin. One night, our former Managing Director, William Kendall, started chatting with the owners of his local Italian deli about the best way to make home-made baked beans. Armed with the right ingredients he set off home to make the recipe, to the despair of his family. This was because, without wanting to be ungrateful, he tends to make inappropriately elaborate suppers which are ready long after bedtime.

Although simple to make, the beans still took hours to cook, giving William the brainwave of selling fresh ready-made bean dishes in cartons for people in a hurry. Here is our version which takes a little over 2 hours if you soak the beans in advance. May you never reach for the canned variety again!

SERVES: 4
PREPARATION AND COOKING TIME: 1-2 hours
Overnight soaking plus 15 minutes

250g (9oz) dried haricot beans, soaked overnight
          in plenty of cold water
1 tablespoon sunflower oil
1 small onion, finely chopped
1 garlic clove, crushed
1 tablespoon black treacle
pinch ground cinnamon
½ teaspoon ground cumin
1 x 400g (14oz) tin chopped tomatoes
1 dessertspoon tomato purée
1 teaspoon English mustard powder
pinch ground cayenne
425ml (3/4 pint) water
½ teaspoon salt
pinch freshly ground black pepper

Drain the haricot beans and rinse in plenty of cold water. Put into a saucepan with the remaining ingredients. Cover, bring to the boil and simmer gently for about 1 hour until the beans are tender. Taste for seasoning.

Captain Beany's
Boston Baked Beans

Captain Beany is a bit of a super hero. He beams himself down from Planet Beanus (somewhere near Port Talbot) to promote and raise money for charity. Beans are his thing. In fact, Captain Beany has turned himself into a human bean for the beany-fit of mankind. His exploits include running a couple of marathons dressed as a runner bean and bathing for 5 cold and excruciating days in baked beans. Luckily his girlfriend, known as Tina Beans, shares his vision. If they marry, no doubt it will be at Gretna Bean!

As you may have gathered Captain Beany is an expert on beans. These sweet, strong and tasty baked beans are a favourite recipe of his, picked up on an interplanetary visit to Boston.

SERVES: 8
PREPARATION TIME: 2 hours 20 minutes
COOKING TIME: 5 hours

Pre-heat the oven to 150°C/300°F/Gas Mark 2

450g (1lb) dried haricot beans
250g (9oz) smoked streaky bacon, cut into lardons
2 tablespoons molasses
1 teaspoon salt
½ teaspoon mustard powder
2 tablespoons dark brown sugar

Put the haricot beans into a large saucepan and cover with lots of water. Bring to the boil over a high heat. Remove from the heat and allow to soak for 1 hour. Drain and return to the saucepan with plenty of water, bring to the boil and simmer gently for about 1 hour or until the beans are tender and the skins beginning to burst. Drain and reserve the cooking liquor.

Put half of the bacon lardons onto the base of an ovenproof casserole dish. Put the beans on top in a single layer. Mix the molasses, salt, dry mustard and brown sugar and spoon over the beans. Add enough of the bean cooking liquor to cover. Sprinkle the remaining bacon lardons on top. Cover and bake for 4½ hours topping up with water if the liquid dries out. Uncover and cook for a final 30 minutes.

Knicky Knocky Baked Beans

Towards the end of the long winters in eastern Canada, the 'sugaring off' season is a welcome highlight, celebrated with festivals, feasts and sleigh rides. 'Sugaring off' is when the sap is collected, with the help of a tap and a bucket, from holes made in the trunks of maple trees. It is then boiled up and turned into irresistibly sweet maple syrup. 40 gallons of sap are used to make just 1 gallon of syrup.

At the celebrations, children love to make maple syrup lollies by rolling 'popsicle' sticks through the boiling syrup poured from jugs straight onto the snow. At the party feasts, which always feature food cooked with maple syrup or maple sugar, pickles are passed around the table between courses to counteract the sweetness. This delightful and addictive sweet and smoky bean dish comes from a sugar bush-the local name for a grove of maples in Knicky Knocky, one of the eastern townships in Quebec. Slightly creamy with a moreish crust, these baked beans are delicious with ham or a piquant green salad.

SERVES: 4
PREPARATION AND COOKING TIME: 5 hours

Pre-heat the oven to 170°C / 325°F / Gas Mark 3

450g (1lb) dry haricot beans
2 litres (3½ pints) water
6 slices bacon or salt pork, about 225g (8oz) cut in pieces
½ large onion, chopped
½ teaspoon dry mustard
100ml (4floz) maple syrup
75ml (3floz) dark rum
570ml (1 pint) bean cooking liquor
2 tablespoons brown sugar
25g (1oz) butter

Put the beans and water into a saucepan, cover, bring to the boil and simmer gently for 2 minutes. Remove from the heat and allow to stand for 1 hour. Return to the boil and simmer gently, covered, for 40 minutes. Drain, reserving the cooking liquor.

Place the bacon or salt pork in an ovenproof dish. Add the beans, onion, mustard, maple syrup, rum and 425ml (3/4 pint) of the reserved cooking liquor. Bake in the oven for 2½ hours in an uncovered pan to allow a crust to form, then add the remaining liquor and bake for a further 30 minutes. Cream together the brown sugar and butter and dot on top. Serve.

Barbecue Beans

(V) (F)

This traditional beans recipe was the brainchild of Gayle Hart, a real food enthusiast who has spent the last 2½ years creating new recipes for us and making sure they work to perfection. We have known Gayle for many years, as she first started working on our show and exhibition stands to earn extra money whilst studying home economics at University. Gayle did lots of research into the origins of American barbecue sauces when looking at new ideas for this dish. Based on a Wild West style of beans from Kansas City, they are both sweet and spicy and are delicious with sausages, chicken legs, or any other meat straight off the 'barbie'.

SERVES: 4
SOAKING TIME: 8 hours
COOKING TIME: 1¼ hours plus overnight soaking

300g (11oz) mixed dried beans, soaked overnight in plenty of cold water
400ml (14 floz) water
1 medium carrot, peeled and cut into 1cm (½") dice
15g (½oz) butter
1 medium onion, finely chopped
1 garlic clove, crushed
110g (4oz) demerara sugar
2 heaped teaspoons wholegrain mustard
1 heaped dessertspoon tomato purée
1 tablespoon soy sauce
100ml (4 floz) cider vinegar
150ml (¼ pint) tomato passata
1 fat red jalapeño chilli, seeded and finely chopped
1 level teaspoon cayenne pepper
pinch of salt
25g (1oz) plain flour

Put the beans into a saucepan with the water, bring to the boil, cover and simmer gently for about 30 minutes, adding more water to cover if necessary, until the beans are tender. Drain and reserve the cooking liquor in a small saucepan, adding the diced carrot. Bring to the boil and simmer gently for about 10 minutes, until the carrot is tender. Drain and reserve the cooking liquor separately.

Meanwhile, heat the butter and cook the onion and garlic gently in a covered saucepan for 5 minutes, without colouring. Add the sugar, mustard, tomato purée and soy sauce, stir well and cook gently for 5 minutes. Stir in the beans, vinegar, passata, chilli, cayenne and salt. Mix the flour with a little of the cooking liquor until smooth and stir this into the bean mixture together with the remaining cooking liquor and diced carrot. Bring to the boil and simmer gently without covering for 20-30 minutes, stirring occasionally.

BEWARE: if the beans are large or old they may need a little extra cooking time.

Southwestern Garbanzo Beans

This American recipe for chickpeas or garbanzo beans, as they call them across the Pond, is delicious. In fact, it has fast become one of our PR Manager, Kate Kime's favourites, having declared it 'a recipe to die for'. Her husband lived off it whilst she was working on this book. The orange coloured, slightly sweet-tasting peas just melt in the mouth and are extremely addictive. Try them hot or cold with rice, warmed naan bread, or just a green herb salad as the perfect comfort food to end a long and busy day.

SERVES: 2
PREPARATION AND COOKING TIME : 35 minutes
1 tablespoon extra virgin olive oil
1 medium onion, finely chopped
1 large garlic clove, finely chopped
1 tablespoon fresh ginger root, finely chopped
250g (9oz) ripe tomatoes, roughly chopped
2 teaspoons ground cumin
1 teaspoon ground coriander
salt and freshly ground black pepper
cayenne pepper to taste
1 x 400g ('14oz) tin of garbanzo beans,
               i.e. chickpeas, drained
150ml (¼ pint) water
1 tablespoon clear honey
110g (4oz) pitted dates, chopped
1 tablespoon lime juice

TO GARNISH:
4 lime wedges
sprigs of fresh coriander

Heat the oil and cook the onion, garlic and ginger for 5 minutes in a covered saucepan, without colouring. Add the tomatoes and cook over a moderate heat, stirring, for 5 minutes. Add the cumin and coriander and season to taste with cayenne, salt and pepper. Cook gently for 1 minute. Add the beans, water, honey and dates. Cover, bring to the boil and simmer gently for 10-15 minutes. Stir in the lime juice and serve in a bowl garnished with lime wedges and sprigs of coriander.

Lima Beans with Chilli & Seed

Lima beans are large, flat and ivory coloured with a pale green tinge. When cooked they have a creamy texture. If you have difficulty finding them, butterbeans, which are in fact a variety of lima beans, make a good substitute. This is great with meat or fish, or just eat them on their own. The sunflower seeds add a good crunchy bite.

SERVES : 2
PREPARATION AND COOKING TIME : 20 minutes

1 tablespoon sunflower oil
1 medium onion, finely chopped
50g (2oz) sunflower seeds, (preferably roasted)
1 tablespoon jalapeño chilli, chopped
1 large tomato, roughly chopped
1 x 400g (14oz) tin of lima or butter beans, drained
salt and freshly ground black pepper
1 tablespoon fresh coriander leaves, chopped

Heat the oil and cook the onion gently for 10 minutes in a covered saucepan without colouring. Stir in the sunflower seeds, tomato, jalapeño chilli and beans. Taste for seasoning. Cook gently for 2 minutes, then stir in the chopped fresh coriander and serve.

Sopa De Arroz
(Dry Rice Soup)

(V) (F)

Cheap and filling lunches are a feature of everyday life in Mexico. In fact, lunch is the main meal and there are little restaurants called 'loncherias' that cater for working people who can't go home to eat. They usually serve a 4-course lunch that may include a pasta soup; a plate of rice cooked with tomatoes and served with a fried egg; refried beans and tortillas followed by rice pudding or crème caramel. Together with a lime drink and coffee, the total cost is around 80p! No wonder they need a siesta afterwards! Sopa de Arroz, meaning Dry Rice Soup isn't actually a soup but a typical, tasty lunchtime rice dish which goes really well with spicy beans.

SERVES: 4
PREPARATION AND COOKING TIME: 40 minutes
Pre-heat oven to its lowest setting

400g (14oz) Basmati rice, well rinsed
6 tablespoons groundnut oil
1 medium onion, finely chopped
2 garlic cloves, finely chopped
2 ripe tomatoes, cut into chunks
1 tablespoon tomato purée
1 litre (1 3/4 pints) vegetable stock (see page 14)
75g (3oz) fresh or frozen peas
75g (3oz) fresh or frozen sweetcorn
75g (3oz) carrots, peeled and finely diced
3 small Thai chillies, deseeded and finely chopped
Salt and freshly ground black pepper

Drain the rice, spread on a baking sheet and put into the oven for 15 minutes to dry. Meanwhile, heat 2 tablespoons of oil in a saucepan and sauté the onion and garlic for 2-3 minutes until soft, then add the tomatoes, tomato purée and a little of the stock and continue cooking for 5 more minutes. Add a little more stock, transfer to a liquidiser and process until smooth. Take the rice out of the oven, add the remaining oil to a saucepan and sauté the rice until golden brown. Drain off the excess oil from the pan, add the tomato mixture and cook vigorously for 1-2 minutes, stirring continuously. Add the peas, sweetcorn, carrots and chillies and the remainder of the vegetable stock. Bring to the boil, then cover and reduce the heat to a simmer for approximately 10 minutes, adding more stock or water if it dries out. Remove from the heat and leave covered for 5 more minutes. Stir well before serving.

Barbados Black Bean Cakes with Mango Sauce

(V) (F)

Once you have tried these bean patties, enlivened by Caribbean spices, you'll want to make them over and over again. Like all bean cakes, they need a sauce, not only to counter their dryness but also to provide a contrast of texture and flavours. This vibrant mango salsa is a wonderful complement to the black bean cakes and provides them with a colourful contrast. For greater effect, garnish with sprigs of fresh coriander and lime wedges and serve with a mixture of grilled vegetables.

SERVES: 2 as starter or light meal
PREPARATION AND COOKING TIME: 40 minutes
400g (14oz) cooked black beans
½ medium red onion, finely chopped
3 garlic cloves, crushed
15g (½oz) fresh coriander leaves, chopped
1 teaspoon ground cumin
½ teaspoon ground allspice
pinch cayenne pepper, or to taste
salt and freshly ground black pepper
1 egg white, lightly beaten and 1 egg, beaten
flour for dusting
110g (4oz) breadcrumbs
oil for frying

FOR THE MANGO SALSA:
1 large ripe mango, cut into fine dice
1 red pepper, seeded and cut into fine dice
½ medium red onion, finely chopped
½ large red chilli, seeded and finely chopped
2 tablespoons fresh coriander leaves, chopped
1 tablespoon lime juice

TO GARNISH:
lime wedges
sprigs of fresh coriander

Combine all the ingredients for the salsa in a bowl, cover and set aside.

Coarsely mash the beans until they stick together. Add the red onion, garlic, coriander, cumin, allspice, cayenne and salt and pepper to taste. Add the egg white and mix well. Divide the mixture into patties. Coat the patties in a dusting of flour, dip in beaten egg and finally breadcrumbs. Heat a little oil in a frying pan and, when hot, add the bean cakes and fry on both sides until golden, about 8 minutes. Serve warm with mango salsa and garnished with lime wedges and sprigs of fresh coriander.

Bean Fritters
with Creamy Shrimp Sauce

(V) (F)

Michael Bateman's recipes make the Independent on Sunday readers' mouths water every week. Whenever possible he combines his love of food and travel with spectacular results. These wonderful bean fritters, served with a creamy, and slightly crunchy, coconut shrimp sauce were a discovery he made in Brazil while researching his book Street Café Brazil. Known as 'acarajé', they are cooked in simmering pans of oil by street vendors in Bahia. Vatapá, the dipping sauce, is also used in the northeast of the country to accompany prawns and poached fish. It takes a while to rub off the skins of the beans, so sit down with a glass of wine and a friend for a chat! The subtly flavoured fritters can be reheated in the oven, though take care they don't dry out.

SERVES: 6 as a main course (5 fritters each)
PREPARATION AND COOKING TIME: Overnight soaking of beans,
30 minutes soaking of dried prawns, plus 1 hour 15 minutes

250g (9oz) black-eyed beans, soaked overnight in plenty of cold water
75g (3oz) dried shrimps (available from Far Eastern delis) soaked overnight in plenty of cold water
1 medium onion
100ml (4floz) water (as needed)
cayenne to taste
salt and freshly ground black pepper
corn oil for deep frying

FOR THE CREAMY SHRIMP SAUCE:
1 tablespoon oil
1 medium onion, finely chopped
1 garlic clove, crushed
25g (1oz) dried shrimps, soaked for 30 minutes in plenty of cold water
15g (½oz) white breadcrumbs
50ml (2floz) coconut cream, sold in small cartons
290ml (½ pint) coconut milk, sold in tins
50g (2oz) skinned almonds
50g (2oz) skinned cashews
1 fresh green chilli, seeded and finely chopped
juice of 1 lime
150ml (¼ pint) fish stock (see page 13)
1 bay leaf
salt and freshly ground black pepper

TO GARNISH:
wedges of fresh lime

Drain and rinse the soaked beans and prawns; rubbing off the bean skins as best you can. Put beans and shrimps in a liquidiser with the onion and purée to a thick paste, adding water as necessary. Add cayenne, salt and pepper to taste. Heat the oil. Take no more than 6 tablespoonfuls of the paste at a time so as not to lower the temperature of the cooking oil and deep fry. When crisp and golden, remove to kitchen paper to drain. Keep hot in a low oven.

To make sauce, heat the oil and cook the onion over a moderate heat for about 10 minutes until beginning to colour, stirring. Add the garlic and cook for a further minute, stirring. Meanwhile, drain the shrimps and put them into a liquidiser with the breadcrumbs, coconut cream, coconut milk, almonds, cashews, green chilli and lime juice. Purée until fairly smooth, then add the mixture to the onions and garlic, together with the fish stock and bay leaf. Taste for seasoning and simmer very gently for 15 minutes to thicken. Taste and adjust seasoning.

Serve the fritters with the sauce on the side and sprinkled with a dribble of lime juice.

Sweet Potato, Sprout & Orange Salad

(V) (F)

The recipe for this fascinating sweet salad with a savoury dressing comes from the South Pacific islands of New Zealand, which in Maori are known as Aotearoa. Jane Rickit, an architect now practising in England, was introduced to its unique flavours by her best friend Emma and feels it best embodies the taste of the long summer evenings of home. In New Zealand, this recipe would include Kumara, an indigenous vegetable very similar in taste to sweet potato. In the salad, the sweetness of the orange and the potatoes is tempered by the lemon juice in the dressing.

SERVES: 4-6
PREPARATION AND COOKING TIME: 35 minutes
475g (1lb 1oz) sweet potato, peeled and cut into 1cm (½") cubes
2 oranges, peeled and cut into segments, without pith
2 shallots, peeled and thinly sliced
175g (6oz) bean sprouts or tinned chickpeas, drained

FOR THE DRESSING:
3 tablespoons groundnut oil
½ teaspoon salt
2 teaspoons ground cumin
1 teaspoon turmeric
2 tablespoons lemon juice
2 tablespoons parsley, finely chopped
freshly ground black pepper

Boil the sweet potato until just cooked, then drain, cool and put into a bowl. Add the orange segments, shallots, and bean sprouts then mix together gently.

Combine the dressing ingredients together in a bowl and whisk well. Season to taste, then pour the dressing over the salad. Toss together lightly. Refrigerate until ready to use. Serve with warm, crusty bread.

Sichuan Green Beans

Sophie Grigson's remarkable recipe for deep-fried green beans is just so good we had to include it amongst our favourites. As she suggests, this is an excellent way of cooking beans even if you don't include all the aromatics. Dried shrimps and Sichuan pepper are readily available in Chinese food shops.

SERVES: 4 as a side-dish or first course
PREPARATION AND COOKING TIME: 35 minutes

2 tablespoons dried shrimps
Vegetable oil for deep frying
450g (1lb) French beans, topped and tailed
2 cloves of garlic, peeled and thinly sliced
½ teaspoon Sichuan or black peppercorns, crushed
2.5cm (1") piece of fresh ginger, peeled and finely chopped
½ teaspoon salt
1 tablespoon sugar
1 tablespoon dark soy sauce
2 tablespoons rice wine vinegar
1 tablespoon sesame oil

Soak the dried shrimp in boiling water for 20 minutes, then drain and reserve the soaking liquid. Chop the shrimp finely and set aside. Half fill a heavy-bottomed saucepan with vegetable oil and heat until hot. Deep fry the beans for 3-4 minutes, until tender, wrinkled and lightly tinged with brown. Remove from the pan and drain on kitchen paper. Place a wok or high-sided frying pan over a medium heat, add 1 tablespoon of vegetable oil and heat until smoke rises. Add the garlic, peppercorns and ginger and stir fry for a few seconds, taking care not to brown them too much. Add the chopped, soaked shrimp and stir-fry for 30 seconds more. Add the salt, sugar, soy sauce and 5 tablespoons of the retained shrimp water. Add the beans, stirring well to ensure they are well coated with the ingredients. Continue to stir until almost all of the liquid has been absorbed and the sauce and the beans have caramelised to a dark brown, almost black colour. Pour in the rice wine vinegar and sesame oil, and stir well to amalgamate the flavours. Serve warm, or even better cold.

Mung Bean Pancakes

Mung beans are popular throughout Asia, and this delectable recipe for little flat pancakes comes from Korea. We recommend that they are best eaten hot or cold with sweet chilli sauce and soy sauce for dipping.

SERVES: 4-6
PREPARATION TIME: 8 hours for bean soaking
                        plus 10 minutes
COOKING TIME: 20 minutes

225g (8oz) dried mung beans, soaked overnight
                in plenty of cold water
170g (6oz) finely diced ham
225g (8oz) shredded Chinese lettuce
1 bunch spring onions, white parts only,
                finely sliced diagonally
2 garlic cloves, crushed
½ teaspoon chilli powder, or to taste
2 eggs, lightly beaten
plenty of salt and freshly ground black pepper
vegetable and sesame oil to fry

Place the soaked beans in a food processor and blend with 100ml (4floz) water to a fairly smooth paste. Stir in the remaining ingredients except the oils and beat well. Heat a little oil and, when hot, drop spoonfuls of the mixture into the pan and cook until golden underneath and small bubbles appear on the surface. Flip over and cook on the other side. Remove to a dish. Repeat with the remaining mixture. Serve either hot or cold with a dipping sauce.

Pune Style Chickpeas

Every Tuesday lunchtime many of us put down our tools and pick up our mats for an hour's yoga practice led by John Shirbon, our superb Iyengar instructor. To many it is a highlight of the week. We emerge feeling capable of tackling any challenge and heartily recommend that other companies introduce such a practice.

The spiritual home of Iyengar yoga is Pune, a vibrant city in western India. When food writer Manisha Gambhir Harkins sent us her aunt Leela's chickpea recipe we had to try it out, especially as Leela originally came from Pune. Manisha tells us that it is a city of 'spicy, fun and colourful people', adjectives which aptly sum up this spectacularly good pulse dish. It's perfect after yoga.

TIP: Tamarind adds a wonderful sour note and is available in paste form at most Indian grocers. A squirt of lemon can be used as a substitute, although the flavour will not be exact.

SERVES: 4
PREPARATION AND COOKING TIME:
Overnight plus 1 hour 10 minutes

225g (8oz) dried chickpeas
2 x 2.5cm (1") slices of fresh root ginger
2 bay leaves
3 cloves
a few black peppercorns
seeds of 5 cardamom pods, ground
1 red chilli, seeded
1 medium onion, roughly chopped
3 garlic cloves, peeled
2 tablespoons vegetable oil
½ teaspoon cumin seeds
¼ teaspoon turmeric
1 cinnamon stick
6 tomatoes, roughly chopped
¼ teaspoon tamarind paste

TO GARNISH:
2 tablespoons fresh coriander leaves, chopped

Soak the chickpeas overnight in plenty of cold water with the ginger, bay leaves, cloves and peppercorns. Drain and rinse in plenty of cold water. Put into a saucepan with 1 Litre (1¾ pints) water, bring to the boil and simmer gently for about 1 hour until tender. Drain, reserving 570ml (1pint) of the cooking liquor and, separately, the ginger and bay leaves.

Put the ground cardamom seeds, reserved bay leaves and ginger, chilli, onion and garlic into a liquidiser with 75ml (3floz) water and purée to a smooth paste. Heat the oil and cook the cumin seeds, turmeric and cinnamon for 30 seconds. Add the onion and spice paste and cook gently for 10 minutes without burning. Add the tomatoes and reserved cooking liquor and cook until the sauce is dark and thick. Finally add the cooked chickpeas, stir and cook for 1 minute. Stir in the tamarind paste and serve garnished with chopped fresh coriander leaves.

Lentil Tart
with Rice Crunch Pastry

Ⓥ

Josceline Dimbleby is known for the inventiveness and originality of her recipes and her unexpected combinations of ingredients. This delicious lentil tart uses ground rice in the pastry and, as it is made with warm butter, it is ideal for cooks with hot hands! Eat warm with a crisp salad and maybe a fresh tomato sauce. It is also great served with home-made tomato soup.

SERVES: 6-8
PREPARATION TIME: 35 minutes   COOKING TIME: 2 hours
Pre-heat oven to 190°C/375°F/Gas Mark 5

FOR THE PASTRY:
170g (6oz) plain flour
1 teaspoon salt
25g (1oz) ground rice
110g (4oz) butter
1 tablespoon water

FOR THE FILLING:
1 onion, finely chopped
175g (6oz) red lentils
570ml (1 pint) of milk
½ teaspoon ground mace
3 pinches chilli powder
salt
1 large egg
50g (2oz) grated Cheddar cheese
paprika to sprinkle

loose bottomed flan tin, approx. 23cm (9")

TO MAKE THE PASTRY:
Sift the flour and salt into a bowl and stir in the ground rice. Put the butter and water into a saucepan and melt the butter gently. Then pour the butter and water mixture into the flour mixture, stirring it in with a wooden spoon to form a warm dough. Press evenly over the base and sides of the flan tin. Refrigerate whilst you make the filling.

TO MAKE THE FILLING:
Put the chopped onion into a saucepan with the lentils and the milk. Simmer very gently in an uncovered pan, stirring occasionally, for 45-60 minutes, until the mixture is thick and mushy. Stir in the ground mace, the chilli powder and the salt. Leave to cool. Whisk the egg and stir into the cooled lentil mixture. Spoon the mixture into the chilled pastry case and sprinkle over the grated cheese. Lastly sprinkle sparingly with paprika and put into the centre of the oven for 35-45 minutes or until the filling has set. Remove the tart from the oven and leave it in the tin for a few minutes. Then very carefully push up the tart out of the tin. Using a long wide spatula, ease the tart off the base of the tin onto a flat, round serving plate.

Dal

The word dal not only refers to the Indian pulse dish, but is also the collective description for the many types of lentils, peas and beans so commonly used in Indian cookery as a source of protein. This is our favourite of the many variations.

Gayle Hart, who works on our new recipes, spared no effort to find the right level and combination of spices to make this authentic-tasting dal. Fortunately for us, we have a real expert in the office. Nina Bahd, who works in our accounts department, grew up in India and is an excellent cook.

Try to use the freshest possible spices and forget about those half empty packets lying at the back of your store cupboard! If you have the time, grind them yourself for a really good flavour. Don't be surprised if you need to add a generous shake of salt; it helps to heighten the flavour of the spices. Serve with naan bread, brushed with butter, and grilled.

SERVES: 4-6
PREPARATION TIME AND COOKING TIME: 45 minutes

50g (2oz) butter
1 large onion, finely chopped
50g (2oz) fresh root ginger, finely grated
1 garlic clove, finely chopped
1 heaped dessertspoon fresh jalapeño chilli, chopped
1 teaspoon ground coriander
1 teaspoon ground cumin
½ teaspoon ground turmeric
¼ teaspoon ground cardamom seed
¼ teaspoon cayenne
¼ teaspoon ground cinnamon
pinch ground cloves
½ teaspoon freshly ground black pepper
pinch freshly ground nutmeg
1.2 litres (2 pints) water
310g (11oz) red lentils, washed twice in plenty of
          cold water and drained
1 x 400g (14oz) tin chopped tomatoes
salt to taste
lemon juice to taste
25g (1oz) fresh coriander leaves, chopped

Heat the butter and cook the onion and ginger gently in a covered saucepan for 5 minutes, without colouring. Add the garlic, chilli and ground spices. Cook gently for 1 minute, stirring. Add the water and lentils. Cover, bring to the boil, and simmer for 10 minutes. Add the tomatoes and taste for seasoning. Cover, bring to the boil and simmer for a further 15 minutes. Add a little more water if the dal is too thick. Just before serving, stir in the lemon juice and coriander.

Paripoo

We discovered this extraordinary recipe from Sri Lanka and just had to include it in the book. Neither salt cod nor pandan leaves are easy to come by, but if you can get them, it's worth the effort. Reminiscent of an exotic and fishy dal, it goes perfectly with rice and curries. The authentic recipe did call for pounded Maldive fish, but as this is very hard to find over here, we used salt cod instead. Pandan leaves can be found in specialist Asian grocery stores.

SERVES: 6
PREPARATION AND COOKING TIME: 1 hour 10 minutes
400g (14oz) red lentils, rinsed
750ml (1¼ pints) water
400ml (14 floz) coconut milk. Separate off 200ml (7floz)
    and thin with 200ml (7floz) water to make
    200ml (7floz) thick coconut milk and
    400ml (14floz) thin coconut milk
1 dried red chilli, finely chopped
60g (2½oz) dried salt cod, soaked in 2 tablespoons
    of milk for 30 minutes, remove any bones
    once soaked
1 teaspoon turmeric
1 tablespoon groundnut oil
6 dried curry leaves
2 medium onions, finely sliced
4cm (2") strip pandan leaf, torn into strips
4cm (2") stick of cinnamon
Small stalk of lemon grass, finely chopped
Salt to taste

Put the lentils into a saucepan with the water, thinned coconut milk, chilli, salt cod and turmeric. Bring to the boil, then turn down the heat and simmer until the lentils are soft. In another pan, heat the oil and fry the curry leaves, onions, pandan leaf, cinnamon and lemon grass until the onions are brown and beginning to crisp. Add half of this mixture to the lentils and reserve half for the garnish. Add the thick coconut milk and salt to taste. Simmer uncovered until the lentils are very soft and the consistency is that of runny porridge.

Kwati

Brontë Barnett was looking forward to a 3 week trekking holiday in Nepal with her best friend, Tessa Sutherland. That was until she discovered she was pregnant and was advised not to go. Her husband Charlie went with the stunningly beautiful Tessa instead, with Brontë's blessing. So while Charlie and Tessa were experiencing the delights of Nepal, Brontë was stuck at home with morning sickness. Although Tessa was a stimulating holiday companion, Charlie missed Brontë terribly and brought her back many tokens of his affection, including a small booklet of local recipes. Brontë sent us Kwati from that booklet, which was in fact the country's 1st published recipe book. Fortunately, the girls still remained best of friends.

According to the author, Nani Hira Kansaker, this recipe, in which the beans are sprouted for an earthy flavour, is prepared for the special festival of Gunepurnima or Kwati Purnima, the Nepali August Full Moon Festival.

SERVES: 4
PREPARATION AND COOKING TIME:
overnight soaking plus 24 hours to sprout beans
                    plus 1 hour 10 minutes

300g (11oz) mixed dried beans (remove broad beans)
2 bay leaves
3/4 teaspoon turmeric
1½ teaspoons cumin
2 teaspoons plain flour
1½ teaspoons omum (ajowan or omum is lovage -
        dried thyme may be substituted)
4 tablespoons extra virgin olive oil
salt

Soak the beans overnight. Drain the water and put the beans in a flat, open dish. Put the dish into a plastic bag pricked with holes, twist the end and tuck under. Leave in a warm place to sprout - the airing cupboard will speed up the process. When just sprouted, wash and put the beans into a saucepan with 850 ml (1½ pints) water. Add all other ingredients except the omum or dried thyme and oil. Cook the beans gently until they are tender. Heat the oil in a separate pan and add the omum or dried thyme. Fry until it is dark, then stir, with the oil, into the cooked beans. Taste for seasoning.

Hot Chickpeas
with Mint Vinaigrette

Pulses are a good alternative to potatoes, rice or pasta, not only because they are cheap, filling, low in fat and high in fibre, but also because they have an unparalleled ability to soak up flavour. Giles Kime, the husband of our PR manager Kate, adores chickpeas. He also has a fine repertoire of recipes that can be made in an instant from basics found in an almost bare kitchen cupboard - fresh herbs from the garden are usually the saviour. He throws together this very easy recipe in a jiffy and eats it with cold sausages or anything else lurking in the back of the fridge. If using tinned chickpeas, this recipe can be made in less than 10 minutes, but the texture and flavour of dried chickpeas is better.

SERVES: 6
PREPARATION AND COOKING TIME: Overnight soaking plus 1 hour 10 minutes (10 minutes if using cooked chickpeas)

400g (14oz) chickpeas, soaked in water overnight and drained
(or can of chickpeas, drained)
1 shallot, peeled and finely chopped
1 tablespoon white wine vinegar
1 tablespoon lemon juice
pinch of sugar
6 tablespoons extra virgin olive oil
handful of fresh mint leaves, roughly torn
salt and freshly ground black pepper

Put the chickpeas into a large saucepan with plenty of water. Bring to the boil, cover, turn down the heat and simmer for 1 hour until cooked but with some bite left to the chickpeas. Drain and set aside. While the chickpeas are cooking, combine the shallot, vinegar, lemon juice and sugar together in a bowl and slowly beat in the olive oil. Pour the hot chickpeas into a bowl and drizzle over the dressing. Toss together with mint leaves and taste for seasoning. Serve immediately whilst still warm.

Lemon Chickpeas With Spinach

We first met professional cook Paul Bloomfield when he made the canapés at the final of one of our competitions - his cooking was superb. With 3 cookery books to his name and the experience of running a restaurant in Dallas, Texas, Paul is an old hand at developing recipes. We asked him to help us test recipes for this book, and it was whilst doing this he created this side dish to go with lamb tagine. The result was so delicious that we decided to ditch the tagine and stick with the chickpeas. Eat them on their own or with lamb, pork or poultry.

SERVES: 4 as a sidedish
PREPARATION AND COOKING TIME : 30 minutes

2 tablespoons of groundnut oil
2.5cm (1") piece of fresh ginger, peeled and finely chopped
3 garlic cloves, peeled and finely minced
1 red chilli, deseeded and finely minced
1 teaspoon ground coriander
1 teaspoon ground cumin
400g (14oz) tin of chickpeas, drained and dried
zest and juice of ½ lemon
400g (14oz) tin of chopped tomatoes
225g (8oz) spinach leaves, washed and roughly chopped
salt and freshly ground black pepper

Heat the oil in a large saucepan over a medium heat and add the ginger, garlic, chilli and spices. Sauté without colouring for 1-2 minutes, stirring well. Take care not to burn. Tip in the chickpeas and lemon zest and stir well. Add the tomatoes. Bring to the boil, then turn down the heat to a simmer. Cook for 15 minutes, then add the spinach and lemon juice and continue cooking for 2-3 minutes until the spinach is tender. Taste for seasoning and serve warm.

Beetroot & Feta Couscous

Gilly Booth squeezed testing a vast number of recipes for this book around her art and film-making. Her meticulous attention to detail was just what we needed to pick out anything confusing or difficult to follow. This is her own contribution, a refreshing combination of Greek salad, beetroot and couscous. It is light and eye-catching. Perfect for a summer lunch in the garden.

SERVES: 4
PREPARATION AND COOKING TIME: 50 minutes
225g (8 oz) couscous
225g (8oz) raw grated beetroot or cooked beetroot, cut into 1cm (½") cubes
3 large tomatoes, diced
½ cucumber, cut into 1cm (½") cubes
1 red onion, peeled and cut into fine dice
4 spring onions, white part only cut diagonally
150g (5oz) Kalamata black olives
225g (8oz) feta cheese

FOR THE DRESSING:
200ml (7floz) extra virgin olive oil
Juice 1 lemon
1 tablespoon balsamic vinegar
½ teaspoon Dijon mustard
3 tablespoons coriander or mint, finely chopped
salt and freshly ground black pepper

Put the couscous into a large bowl until just covered with boiling water, stir frequently for 5-10 minutes whilst the water is being absorbed to prevent lumps forming. Add the remaining salad ingredients to the couscous and combine together well. Refrigerate for 30 minutes.

Whisk all of the dressing ingredients together in a bowl and then drizzle over the couscous. Taste for seasoning and serve.

Israeli Fala[fel]

Many of us have our own falafel recipes, bu[t this is the]
favourite of Micah Caw-Hill, one of our de[...]
Taken from Jane Grigson's Vegetable Boo[k ...]
brown and crunchy on the outside and [...]
pretty green on the inside. The texture is [...]
crunchy and not too dry. They can be a [...]
depending on how much cayenne peppe[r ...]
prefer them hot. Try stuffing them, Mid[...]
into a pitta bread pocket, with salad a[nd]
yoghurt. Alternatively, try your hand at [...]
food by serving them with a citrus sa[...]
our salsas (see page 147-148).

MAKES 12 FALAFEL
PREPARATION AND COOKING TIME:
24 hours soaking the chickpeas plus 1 hour 2[...]

110g (4oz) dried chickpeas, soaked for 24 hours
    in plenty of cold water
1 small onion, roughly sliced
1 large garlic clove, peeled and halved
15g (½oz) fresh flat leaf parsley, chopped
15g (½oz) fresh coriander, chopped including s[...]
1 teaspoon ground cumin
1 teaspoon ground coriander
cayenne to taste
salt and freshly ground black pepper
¼ level teaspoon baking powder
oil for deep frying

In a food processor, reduce the chickpea[s, ...]
the onion, garlic, parsley and corianc[...]
the mixture is reduced to a paste f[...]
falafel to hold together in the pan. [...]
experiment a little but it's worth it! [...]
and cayenne, salt and pepper to ta[...]
baking powder. Cover and leave for[...]
refrigerator.

Form the paste into walnut-sized ba[...]
pushing out any extra moisture. He[...]
frying pan, until very hot. Then dee[p fry...]
at a time. If you cook too many a[...]
of the oil will drop, making the balls[...]
become greasy. Fry the balls until [...]
and crunchy on the outside. Drain [...]
Serve hot.

Spicy Vegetable Couscous (V)

Eleanor Cotter, a committed foodie, is on a personal mission
to try any good new restaurant in London almost before
the paint has dried on its door. She worked on our behalf
for 3 years at Phipps PR, our public relations consultancy.
Now she works for HM Government on a variety of projects
from recruitment drives for the Air Force to an initiative to
prevent children suffering burns. Because of her vegetarian
background, Eleanor probably spends more time than most
looking for different ways to cook with vegetables. She gave
us this one after a passionate phase of exploring North
African style cuisine.

SERVES: 4-6
PREPARATION AND COOKING TIME: 30 minutes

400g (14oz) couscous
4 tablespoons extra virgin olive oil
3 shallots, peeled and finely chopped
1 yellow pepper, de-seeded and finely chopped
1 red pepper, de-seeded and finely chopped
1 courgette, finely cubed
110g (4oz) mushrooms, quartered
6 sun-dried tomatoes, finely chopped
1 tablespoon dried chilli flakes, crushed
1 tablespoon dry sherry
2 tablespoons tomato purée
12 cherry tomatoes, halved
salt and pepper, to taste

TO GARNISH:
toasted pine nuts

Put the couscous into a large bowl and add boiling water
until barely covered. Stir frequently for 5-10 minutes whilst
the water is being absorbed, to prevent lumps forming.
Heat the olive oil in a heavy bottomed pan and add the
shallots. Sauté without colouring. Add the peppers and
courgette, stir well and add the mushrooms. Cook for
2 to 3 minutes. Add the sun-dried tomatoes, chilli flakes
and tomato purée and cook for a few minutes more.
Add the sherry and cherry tomatoes and cook for
another 5 minutes. Stir this mixture well through the
couscous, season and garnish with toasted pine nuts.

Sweet Cous

Books for Cooks is a wonderful specialist b[ook]
the helpful staff will find you a book on e[very]
could dream of. We often attend their cool[ery]
workshops, and it was at Anissa Helou's de[monstration of]
food, that we acquired this recipe, includ[ing]
Café Morocco. Anissa explains that it is o[ne of the]
almost sweet dishes that the Moroccans [serve as]
desserts (before the puddings). Even thou[gh, at]
the end of a meal, they are not quite [...]
serving sweet couscous for breakfast. W[e think it's a]
good idea-believe us, it is. A large bowlf[ul shared with a group]
of friends on a Sunday morning is a pe[rfect alternative to]
a fry-up.

TIP: We have used pre-cooked couscous b[ut you can use]
regular couscous. Prepare it by moisten[ing]
350ml (14floz) to 450g (1lb) of regular co[uscous with a teaspoon]
of salt. Work the water in gradually u[...]
the couscous with a tablespoon of oliv[e oil and leave]
covered for 25 minutes.

SERVES: 4
PREPARATION AND COOKING TIME: 25 [minutes]

340g (12oz) couscous
50g (2oz) unsalted butter
150g (5oz) blanched almonds
3 tablespoons icing sugar

TO GARNISH:
ground cinnamon

Prepare the couscous according to [the instructions on the]
packet; set aside. Meanwhile, pu[t the butter in a pan]
and sauté the almonds until g[olden. Remove from]
the pan and leave to cool, the[n] [grind the]
almonds in a ~~food~~ processor. [Reserve a little]
for garnish. Stir the ground a[lmonds and icing sugar]
through the warm couscous a[nd pile into a]
mound. Sprinkle ground cinn[amon and the reserved]
across the couscous, then line[...]
cinnamon trails. Serve imme[diately with more icing]
sugar, if you prefer.

Lamb & Pork with Walnuts, Pumpkin, Prunes & White Beans

This good, hearty stew, ideal for a kitchen supper with friends, is a masterful concoction from cookery writer Lee Bailey. Based on the lamb stews popular in Russia's southern provinces, Lee's version has struck exactly the right balance between the meat, vegetables, beans, nuts and dried fruits.

SERVES: 4-6
PREPARATION AND COOKING TIME: 1 hour 30 minutes

25g (1oz) butter
1 tablespoon extra virgin olive oil
675g (1½lb) boned leg of lamb, cut into 2.5cm (1") cubes
340g (12oz) pork, cut into smaller cubes
2 medium onions, roughly chopped
2 teaspoons salt
½ teaspoon freshly ground black pepper
2 tablespoons sugar
400ml (14floz) beef stock (see page 11) or
    1 tin of beef consommé
16 pitted prunes
450g (1lb) pumpkin or butternut squash,
    peeled and cut into 2.5cm (1") cubes
110g (4oz) walnuts, roughly chopped
1 x 400g (14oz) tin cannellini beans, drained
3 tablespoons fresh coriander leaves, chopped

Heat the butter and oil and brown a few pieces of lamb and pork at a time over a high heat taking care not to over brown. If you add too many pieces, there will be too much moisture and the lamb will stew. Set aside the browned meat and cook the onions gently in the same fat for 5 minutes until beginning to soften. Add the salt, pepper, sugar and stock. Return the meat to the pan, bring to the boil, cover and simmer gently for 30 minutes. Add the prunes and pumpkin. Cover, bring to the boil and simmer gently for 20 minutes or until the pumpkin is just tender and not falling apart. Carefully stir in the walnuts and beans, cover and simmer gently for a further 10 minutes. Stir in most of the chopped fresh coriander leaves and serve sprinkled with the remainder.

Armenian Lentil & Bulgar Cakes

This Armenian dish is a vegetarian 'Kibbeh' using lentils in place of meat. The colourful yellow cakes, flecked with red and green peppers, are just as good if made with couscous rather than bulgar wheat. Try them with Mango Pica-de-Gallo (see page 148), or a cucumber and tomato salad.

SERVES: 6
PREPARATION AND COOKING TIME: 1hour 15 minutes
110g (4oz) red lentils
425ml (3/4 pint) water
1 teaspoon salt
110g (4oz) butter
75g (3oz) bulgar wheat
1 medium onion, finely chopped
½ medium red pepper, seeded and finely chopped
½ medium green pepper, seeded and finely chopped
1 bunch of spring onions, white part only, finely chopped
2 tablespoons fresh flat leaf parsley, chopped
1 teaspoon paprika
2 tablespoons fresh mint, chopped
salt and freshly ground black pepper
1 tablespoon oil for frying

Put the lentils, water and salt into a large saucepan. Bring to the boil, then simmer gently for about 20 minutes until the lentils are tender. Add more hot water if needed. Stir in 75g (3oz) of the butter and the bulgar wheat. Simmer gently for a further 2 minutes. Remove from the heat, cover, and set aside for 15 minutes.

Meanwhile, melt the remaining butter and fry the onion over a moderate heat for about 10 minutes until the onions are golden, stirring frequently. In a large bowl, combine the onion, lentil and bulgar wheat mixture. Add the red and green peppers, spring onions, parsley, paprika and mint and mix well. Dipping hands occasionally into a bowl of warm water, knead the mixture for about 2 minutes until well blended. Taste for seasoning. Form the mixture into patties.

Heat the oil and fry the patties on both sides over a moderate heat until golden.

Spicy Vegetable Garden Hot Pot (V)

Every working day Linda Jamieson cooks lunch for the 30 partners of a London firm of solicitors, in addition to their numerous dinners, breakfasts and seminars. Several of them are vegetarians so she is always concocting new recipes to add to her repertoire. We think Linda should offer this one to the vegetarian Society as a secret weapon. It's enough to make the most hardened carnivore waver at a meal! Eat on its own, with bread or rice. This is the perfect recipe for a weekend of feeding hungry people, as it keeps well when made 24 hours in advance.

SERVES: 6
PREPARATION AND COOKING TIME: 60 minutes
2 tablespoons extra virgin olive oil
1 red onion, sliced
1 garlic clove, crushed
1 teaspoon Madras curry powder
1 teaspoon ground cumin
¼ teaspoon ground cardamom seeds
¼ teaspoon ground nutmeg
pinch of ground allspice
1 tablespoon fresh root ginger, finely grated
1 large red chilli, seeded and finely sliced
1 tablespoon wholemeal flour
425ml (¾ pint) vegetable stock (see page 14)
1 bunch baby carrots, cut in half lengthways, retaining
       a little of the green tops
460g (1lb) butternut squash, peeled and cut into 2.5cm (1") cubes
250g (9oz) celery, sliced
450g (1lb) fresh broad beans, removed from the pods
1 x 425g (15oz) tin butter beans, drained
2 tablespoons fresh coriander leaves, chopped
lemon juice to taste
salt and freshly ground black pepper

TO GARNISH:
150ml (¼ pint) natural yoghurt
50g (2oz) toasted cashew nuts

Heat the oil and cook the red onion over a moderate heat for about 10-15 minutes until caramelised. The red colour will fade and the onions will take on a brownish hue. Add the garlic and cook gently for 2 minutes. Stir in the curry powder, cumin, cardamom, nutmeg, allspice, ginger and chilli and cook gently for a further 2 minutes. Add the wholemeal flour and stir for 2 minutes over a gentle heat. Gradually add the stock, bring to the boil, and simmer gently for 2 minutes.

Add the baby carrots, butternut squash and celery, and cook gently for 5 minutes. Add the broad beans and butter beans, and cook gently for a further 3-4 minutes or until the vegetables are tender. Just before serving, add the fresh coriander leaves and stir gently. Add lemon juice, salt and pepper to taste. Serve garnished with spoonfuls of natural yoghurt and sprinkled with cashew nuts.

Sausage &
Cabbage Housh

Housh, the invention of Stella Waldron, is an original word for an original recipe. She explains it as a dish of whatever tastes good that goes together well. Stella, the sister of one of our recipe testers, thought up this very moreish, chunky meal-in-one when she became frantically bored with her husband Alastair's allergy diet which excluded wheat, potatoes and cheese. 'As flexible as a bungee jump' is how she describes it because the ingredients can be changed. Try pieces of chicken, strips of pork merguez or chunks of lamb instead of sausage, or substitute the meat with chunky vegetables. Stella often adds Worcestershire sauce, a dash of Maggi or other seasoning, depending on her mood. Serve with lashings of grated cheese and bread for those not on strict exclusion diets.

SERVES: 6-8
PREPARATION AND COOKING TIME: 45 minutes
450g (1lb) good pure pork sausages
2 tablespoons extra virgin olive oil
2 large red onions, finely sliced
225g (8oz) hot chorizo sausage, cut into chunks
1 x Mattesson's smoked pork horseshoe sausage, sliced diagonally
1 x 400g (14oz) tin flageolet beans, drained
1 x 400g (14oz) tin cannellini beans, drained
3 x 400g (14oz) tin chopped tomatoes
150ml (¼ pint) lamb stock (see page 10)
1 tablespoon tomato purée, optional
salt and freshly ground black pepper
450g (1lb) cabbage, shredded

Pre-heat the grill. Grill the pure pork sausages until brown, turning occasionally. Cool and slice thickly diagonally. Heat the oil and fry the onions for 5 minutes. Turn up the heat and add the chorizo, frying for 2 minutes, and then the sliced horseshoe sausage, frying until it begins to brown. Add the flageolet and cannellini beans and grilled sausages and heat through. Add the chopped tomatoes, lamb stock, tomato purée and taste for seasoning. Cover, bring to the boil and simmer gently for 5 minutes.

Meanwhile, half fill a large saucepan with water, cover and bring to the boil. Take off the heat and throw in the shredded cabbage. Stir for 15 seconds, then drain well, reserving some of the cooking liquor in case you need to let down the housh. Stir the cabbage into the housh mixture, taste for seasoning and serve piping hot.

Broad Beans with Pancetta & Cherry Tomatoes

Julia Laflin, who has worked with us for 5 years, spent many hours when we were writing this book rifling through all the recipes we have collected over the years.
One morning, tired and hungry, she headed for the kitchen. Swapping pen for pan, she dreamt up this simple and colourful bean dish, based on the classic Italian broad bean and ham recipe.

These beans are a delicious light meal, served warm or at room temperature - either on their own or with fresh bread.

SERVES 4
PREPARATION AND COOKING TIME : 15 minutes

250g (9oz) fresh or frozen broad beans (podded weight)
1-2 tablespoons olive oil
1 medium red onion, chopped
1-2 garlic cloves, chopped
175g (6oz) pancetta, roughly chopped
1 dessertspoon tomato purée
225g (8oz) small cherry tomatoes, halved
1-2 teaspoons dried herbes de Provence
salt and freshly ground black pepper

Steam the broad beans until tender, drain and cover. Meanwhile heat oil and cook onion in frying/sauté pan for about 3 minutes, without colouring. Add garlic and continue cooking for another couple of minutes over a gentle heat.

Add the pancetta and tomato purée to the onions and continue cooking until the pancetta is cooked. Add the cherry tomatoes and herbes de Provence and cook slowly for a further 2 minutes. Add the broad beans and continue to cook for another 2-3 minutes, until the tomatoes soften slightly, but still retain their shape.

Season to taste.

Tuscan Beans

One of our bestselling recipes is Tuscan Bean soup. We receive a stream of anxious letters checking if we still make it, whenever people can't find it in their local supermarket or grocers. Reminiscent of a classic Italian bean soup, its strong Mediterranean flavours remind people of local Italian restaurants and Tuscan holidays. Micah Caw-Hill, a food science student on work placement with us, decided it could be reworked into an excellent bean dish. Whilst not very original, the finished result more than made up for it. There are many who even prefer it to the soup. Eat with a chunk of bread, grilled meat or a baked potato.

SERVES : 4
PREPARATION AND COOKING TIME : overnight plus 55 minutes

250g (9oz) mixed dried beans, soaked overnight
        in plenty of cold water
1 tablespoon olive oil
1 small onion, finely chopped
1 garlic clove, crushed
1 leek, washed and finely sliced
½ red pepper, seeded and finely chopped
75g (3oz) button mushrooms, finely chopped
½ teaspoon dried oregano
170g (6oz) tomato passata
2 tablespoons fresh flat leaf parsley, chopped
75g (3oz) peas
salt and freshly ground black pepper

Drain the beans and rinse in plenty of cold water. Put the beans into a saucepan with plenty of water and simmer for about 45 minutes until they are tender. Meanwhile, heat the oil and cook the onion, garlic and leek for 5 minutes in a covered saucepan, without colouring. Add the red pepper and button mushrooms and cook gently for 5 minutes, uncovered. Add the oregano, passata, parsley and peas. Taste for seasoning. Stir in the beans, cover and cook gently for a further 10 minutes.

Karen's Speedy Courgette & Bacon Risotto

Karen Jones, who combines selling our soup to caterers, a long commute to the office and an impressive fitness regime, is also a keen rider and manages to spend most weekends eventing her horse, Henry. When she cooks it has to be tasty, healthy and quick to prepare - hence her love of risottos. Tiring of a mushroom recipe, she graduated to bacon and broad beans before settling on her current favourite, courgette and bacon. Keen on courgettes, she even has her own supply. Her father frequently drops them off by the basketful from his garden. Karen's simple and moreish risotto is perfect after lots of fresh air and exercise.

SERVES: 2
PREPARATION AND COOKING TIME: 25 minutes
1 tablespoon olive oil
2 shallots, peeled and finely chopped
1 clove of garlic, finely chopped
110g (4oz) streaky bacon, finely chopped
175g (6oz) courgettes, thinly sliced
175g (6oz) Arborio rice
425ml (3/4 pint) chicken stock (see page 9)
150ml (1/4 pint) white wine
2 tablespoons double cream
2 tablespoons parsley, finely chopped

Heat the oil in a heavy bottomed saucepan, then add the shallots, garlic and bacon and sauté for 3 to 4 minutes. Then add the courgettes and cook for 2 to 3 minutes more. Add the rice and combine well with the other ingredients. Add the white wine and stock in small quantities, stirring to incorporate each addition with the rice, until it is plump with a bite. Then stir in the double cream and parsley.
Serve immediately.

Seafood Risotto

Jo Gilks is a superb cook who has tested hundreds of recipes for us over the years and, however pernickety we are, she always manages a cheerful smile. Three of us regularly appear at her tranquil garden flat to test her efforts – a peaceful haven and a far cry from our often frenetic office. Jo gave us this wonderfully impressive, yet uncomplicated, version of seafood risotto which follows the more liquid style of risottos favoured by the Venetians. The list of seafood ingredients may seem extravagant but they should easily be found in any good fishmongers. The expense is justified by the worthwhile result.

SERVES: 4
PREPARATION AND COOKING TIME: 1 hour 15 minutes
170g (6oz) cooked prawns, peeled and shells retained
2 shallots, sliced
4 garlic cloves, finely chopped
a few parsley stalks
150ml (¼ pint) water
150ml (¼ pint) dry white wine
450g (1lb) mussels, scrubbed and washed several times
             in plenty of cold water, beards removed
450g (1lb) small clams, scrubbed and washed several
             times in plenty of cold water
1.5 litres (2½ pints) fish stock (approx.) (see page 13)
4 tablespoons sunflower oil
1 large onion, very finely chopped
225g (8oz) risotto rice, preferably Carnaroli
225g (8oz) squid, cleaned and cut into 2.5cm (1") pieces
salt and freshly ground black pepper
2 tablespoons fresh flat leaf parsley, chopped

TO GARNISH:
1 tablespoon sunflower oil
8 large scallops, trimmed of the surrounding white muscle
pinch of salt
1 tablespoon fresh flat leaf parsley, chopped

Put the prawn shells into a large saucepan with the shallots, ¼ of the garlic, parsley stalks, water and wine. Cover and bring to the boil. Add the mussels and clams, cover and cook over a high heat for about 3 minutes or until all the shells have opened. Strain the cooking liquor into a bowl, and discard the prawn shells. When cool enough to handle, remove the shells from ⅔ of the mussels and clams. Set shellfish aside to cool, then cover and chill. Strain the cooking liquor through muslin or a very fine sieve and put into a saucepan with the fish stock and bring to the boil. Simmer gently.

Heat the oil in a large frying pan and cook the onion and remaining garlic gently for 10 minutes until soft, without colouring. Add the rice and stir for 30 seconds, making sure the rice doesn't catch on the base of the pan. Add a ladleful of simmering stock and stir very regularly with a gentle action until the stock has become totally absorbed before another ladleful of stock is added. Keep adding the stock in this way for about 10 minutes, when the rice should be half cooked. Gently stir in the shellfish and squid, taste for seasoning, and continue to add stock until the rice is tender but still retains a bite. Remove the pan from the heat and stir in the parsley.

Quickly prepare the garnish. Heat the oil and sauté the scallops and a pinch of salt over a high heat until lightly browned and cooked through, about 2 minutes. Spoon the risotto onto warmed plates and serve garnished with the scallops and a sprinkling of chopped parsley.

Risotto with Leeks, Broad Beans & Rocket

Risottos tend to feature heavily on the menu at Micah Caw-Hill's house. Once a week he makes a stock with the carcass of his chicken or guinea fowl roast, every inch of which is put to good use, except for the parson's nose! A good stock is vital to this rich and cheesy recipe. Micah, one of our talented students, recommends experimenting with a variety of risotto ingredients but cautions that it is better to have fewer distinctive flavours, than too many different ones. 'Don't stint on the butter and Parmesan as these give the dish its richness,' is his advice.

SERVES: 4-6
COOKING AND PREPARATION TIME: 1 hour 30 minutes
250g (9oz) fresh broad beans, shelled (approx 1K in their pods)
110g (4oz) unsalted butter
3 tablespoons double cream
4 tablespoons flat leaf parsley, chopped
1 tablespoon lemon juice, freshly squeezed
2 tablespoons olive oil
4 leeks, white part only, thinly sliced
400g (14oz) Arborio rice
200ml (⅓ pint) dry white wine
1litre (1¾ pints) chicken stock (see page 9)
300g (11oz) rocket
110g (4oz) Parmesan cheese, freshly grated
salt and freshly ground black pepper

Boil the broad beans in salted water for 5 minutes. Drain and refresh, then peel off their tough skins. Add ⅓ of the butter to a saucepan over a medium heat. Add the broad beans and cover. Cook for 5 minutes. Add the cream and cook for 5 minutes more, then add ½ the parsley and lemon juice and taste for seasoning. Set this aside until later.

Melt the next ⅓ of butter, with the olive oil, in a saucepan. Add the leeks and cook for 2-3 minutes. Then add the rice and stir well to coat with the butter and olive oil. Stirring continuously, add the white wine gradually, then ladle by ladle, add the stock, ensuring the liquid is absorbed before each addition. Continue to do this until the rice is cooked but still has bite. Stir in the bean mixture, rocket, Parmesan cheese and remaining butter. Cook for 2-3 minutes more, until the rocket has just wilted. Add the rest of the parsley. Serve immediately.

Chicken Liver
& Mushroom Risotto

Sue Lawrence has the enviable job of writing about food for the Sunday Times from her home in Scotland. She has given us a recipe which not only tastes but also looks terrific. When we asked her about the idea behind her recipe she confessed that gin and tonic is one of her favourite tipples, so naturally she is fond of the juniper berries that give gin its unique flavour. The risotto was built around the special taste of these berries. Whenever Sue cooks it, she finds the smell released by crushing the berries with a pestle and mortar is so gin-like that it tempts her into pouring herself a long G and T!

SERVES: 4

PREPARATION AND COOKING TIME: 30 minutes

25g (1oz) butter
3 tablespoons extra virgin olive oil
1 medium onion, finely chopped
1 garlic clove, crushed
340g (12oz) button mushrooms, finely sliced
grated zest of 1 lemon
20-30 juniper berries, crushed
salt and freshly ground black pepper
340g (12oz) Arborio, or other risotto rice
290ml (½ pint) dry white wine
750-850ml (1¼-1½ pints) simmering hot
           chicken stock (see page 9)
450g (1lb) chicken livers, washed and drained
50g (2oz) Parmesan cheese, freshly grated

Heat the butter and 1 tablespoon of the oil in a large covered saucepan and cook the onion and garlic gently for 5 minutes, without colouring. Add the mushrooms, lemon zest and half the juniper berries. Taste for seasoning and cook gently for 2 minutes. Add the rice and stir for 30 seconds, making sure the rice doesn't catch on the base of the pan. Increase the heat and add the wine. Cook for 2 minutes, stirring, then lower the heat. Add a ladleful of simmering stock and stir gently until it has become totally absorbed before adding another ladleful. Keep adding the stock in this way until the rice is just tender and the stock absorbed.

Meanwhile, towards the end of cooking time, heat the remaining oil in a frying pan until very hot and add the chicken livers and remaining juniper berries. Add a little seasoning and cook over a high heat for 2-3 minutes, stirring, until the livers are well browned but still pink inside. Stir most of the Parmesan cheese into the risotto and adjust the seasoning. Spoon onto warmed plates. Top with the chicken livers and pour over the juices from the pan. Sprinkle with the remaining Parmesan cheese and serve at once.

Butternut Squash Risotto

If the most recent additions to your family are small, noisy and sleep-depriving but a joy to be with when happy and sweet-smelling, you probably have very young children. As a father of twin girls, Mark Hix, executive Head Chef of Caprice Holdings which includes the Ivy, Le Caprice and Sheekey restaurants in London, had to rethink his approach to cooking at home. While wanting his children to grow up loving food that is both freshly prepared and wholesome, he also likes to cook meals that they all can enjoy together.

Similar to a normal risotto, this loose and milky version of his is perfect for young tummies. It is wine-free, has no salt to strain a baby's kidney and contains plenty of full cream milk. The good thing is, it is just as nice for grown-ups!

SERVES: 2 adults / 6-8 babies
PREPARATION AND COOKING TIME : 30 minutes

500ml (17½fl oz) vegetable stock (see page 14)
1 butternut squash - approximately 500g (1lb 2oz),
          peeled and diced
1 dessertspoon olive oil
150g (5oz) Arborio or Carnaroli rice
200ml (7fl oz) full cream milk
2 tablespoons fresh parsley, chopped
25g (1oz) Parmesan cheese, freshly grated

Bring the stock to the boil, then add the squash and cook for 3-4 minutes until tender. Remove the squash with a slotted spoon and pour the stock into a heatproof jug. Set aside. Heat the oil in a large heavy bottomed saucepan, then add the rice and stir well for 30 seconds. Add the stock in small quantities, about ½ cup at a time, stirring well over a medium heat. Each quantity of stock needs to be almost absorbed before the next addition. Continue until the rice is soft and just cooked through; the rice grains should be plump but with a slight bite left to them. Add the cooked squash, milk and parsley and stir well. Simmer for 5 minutes. Remove from the heat. Sprinkle on the Parmesan and serve immediately.

Bacon, Mozzarella & Avocado Kedgeree

There are times when only something warm and stodgy will do. Usually it's winter and the contents of the fridge have endless possibilities, but in summer, a few salad ingredients don't look quite so hopeful. Kate Kime, who handles our public relations, often finds herself faced with an odd selection. A great fan of the traditional Kedgeree, she tends to experiment with anything else to hand. Anything will do - mix and match according to what you have and what you feel like eating!

SERVES: 4
PREPARATION AND COOKING TIME: 30 minutes

570ml (1 pint) chicken stock (see page 9)
225g (8oz) Basmati rice, washed and rinsed
        3 times in plenty of cold water
a pinch of salt
200g (7oz) smoked bacon, rind and fat removed
50g (2oz) butter
1 bunch spring onions, white parts only, sliced
2 ripe avocados, cut into 1cm (1/2") dice
4 tablespoons crème fraîche
2 x mozzarella, sliced
handful of fresh basil leaves, chopped
salt and freshly ground black pepper

TO GARNISH:
reserved grilled bacon slices (see method)
handful fresh basil leaves

Put the stock into a large saucepan, cover and bring to the boil. Add the rice and salt. Simmer gently for about 10 minutes until the rice is tender. Drain. Meanwhile, grill the bacon until crisp. Chop all but 4 slices, keeping the remaining 4 slices warm.

Heat the butter and add the chopped bacon and spring onions. Cook for 1 minute. Add the avocado and gently warm through, ensuring the avocado still holds its shape. Take the contents out of the pan with a slotted spoon - keep aside. Add the rice, crème fraîche, mozzarella and basil to the pan and warm through. Taste for seasoning. Turn onto a plate and spoon the avocado and bacon mixture on top. Top with slices of the crispy bacon and basil. Accompany with a tomato salad.

Cannellini Beans with Sage

In Tuscany, this dish is Known as 'fagioli all'uccelletti', which means 'beans made the little birds' way'. According to Italian food expert and writer Anna Del Conte, whose work we admire greatly, this is because 'uccelletti' - little birds - are the traditional accompaniment. Needless to say, the beans go well with poultry and game birds too. We have added a dash of white wine and, if you have time, try using dried rather than tinned beans (they'll need to be soaked overnight and cooked for approximately 1½ hours or according to directions on the packet) for greater depth of flavour.

SERVES: 4
PREPARATION AND COOKING TIME: 40 minutes
2 x 400g (14oz) tins of cannellini beans, drained
2 tablespoons olive oil
bay leaf
2 fresh sprigs of thyme or winter savory
10 fresh sage leaves
1 medium onion, roughly chopped
3 garlic cloves, finely chopped
75ml (3 floz) dry white wine
salt and freshly ground black pepper

TO GARNISH:
1 tablespoon fresh flat leaf parsley, chopped

Put the beans into a saucepan with 1 tablespoon olive oil, the bay leaf, thyme and 2 of the sage leaves, cover and warm gently until you need them.

Heat the remaining tablespoon of olive oil and cook the onion gently for 5 minutes in a covered saucepan, without colouring. Add the remaining sage leaves and garlic, cover and cook gently for 10 minutes. Add the wine and cook gently for another minute. Add the bean mixture, taste for seasoning, cover and cook gently for a further 20 minutes. If necessary, add a little water to Keep the mixture just moist. Serve sprinkled with chopped fresh parsley.

Cannellini Beans with Lemony Dill Sauce

This fresh, yet creamy, lemony dill sauce transforms the cannellini beans. We would eat them, as Josceline Dimbleby suggests, with bread and salad, or with pork, veal or grilled fish.

SERVES: 2
PREPARATION AND COOKING TIME:
Overnight soak plus 1 hour 15 minutes

170g (6oz) dried cannellini beans, soaked overnight
in plenty of cold water
2 tablespoons olive oil

FOR THE SAUCE:
150ml (¼ pint) double cream
the juice and zest of 1 lemon, finely grated
handful of fresh dill, finely chopped
salt and freshly ground black pepper

Drain the beans and put into a saucepan with plenty of water. Bring to the boil and simmer for 30-50 minutes (older pulses will take longer) until they are soft but not breaking up. Drain and put into a warm serving bowl. Stir in the olive oil and keep warm while you make the sauce.

To do this, put the cream and the lemon zest into a saucepan. Bring to the boil and bubble, stirring for 2 minutes. Remove pan from the heat and gradually stir in the lemon juice, followed by the chopped dill. Taste for seasoning. Mix the sauce into the cooked beans and serve immediately.

Pease Pottage

We have already mentioned our association with the National Trust in the Mulligatawny Soup recipe. Flatford Mill, one of its best known properties, is in Constable country on the sleepy River Stour. Here, you can eat a relaxing lunch or tea surrounded by flowers, birds and animals. At the Mill's candlelit suppers, the menus have a historic theme and Pease Pottage is always a winter favourite. This recipe is taken from The National Trust Recipes Book.

Apparently, in the Middle Ages, pottage was the term used for a semi-liquid mess of food. Vegetable pottages, like this one, were for the poor while the rich dined on spicy meat or fish pottage. If this was only a pauper's dish, we should be searching the Trust's recipe archives for more! It is a luxurious, liquidy alternative to plain vegetables and its minty sweetness is terrific with baked gammon, roast lamb or chops.

SERVES: 4
PREPARATION TIME: 5 minutes
COOKING TIME: 30 minutes
450g (1lb) frozen peas
110g (4oz) butter
1 tablespoon fresh mint, chopped
1 teaspoon sugar
salt and freshly ground black pepper
1 tablespoon single cream

Defrost the peas and place in a saucepan with the butter. Cover and cook slowly over a medium to low heat for 20-25 minutes until they become mushy. Stir in the mint and cook for 3 minutes. Add the sugar and taste for seasoning. Swirl in the cream just before serving.

Breads

Breads

Bread is hugely under-rated. Whilst you can now buy a larger variety of breads than ever before, there is nothing quite like an all natural home-made loaf straight from the oven. As it doesn't contain preservatives, home-made bread doesn't last as long as bought, but if you're making for a family or a group of friends it needn't matter - it will all go! It also tends to freeze well.

Many people are wary of making bread, thinking it is tricky and laborious. Whilst some breads are indeed more complicated, there are so many recipes that are not only terribly simple, but also delicious. The one common thread from all our favourite recipes is their simplicity. If you have never made bread before, now is the time to try! Some of these recipes take just minutes of work, and others don't even need to rise or prove.

As long as you use an oven- or fireproof dish, you need not be confined to baking bread in a loaf tin - use whatever you want to make a variety of different shaped loaves.

There are a few guidelines to remember, but once you've got those mastered, it's easy!

— Salt is important, but don't add too much as it will slow down the rising time

— Always make sure your hands, and the surface you knead on, are as cold as possible. A marble slab is ideal

— Kneading helps to distribute the yeast and gives the dough its elasticity. Push the dough down and away from you using the heel of your hand, then pull it back with your fingers and bang it down on the surface, rotating the dough a little each time. You should knead until the dough is no longer sticky, but smooth, elastic and shiny

— Rising can be speeded up by putting the dough in a warm place, but the longer the dough is left to rise naturally at room temperature, the better the bread. Dough can be left to rise in the lowest part of the fridge, but it takes about 10-12 hours. Perfect when preparing in advance

— To knock back, punch any large airholes out of the dough with your knuckles. This will reduce the risen dough back to its original size. A quick kneading then makes it pliable

— Proving is the second rising of the dough. It makes bread (particularly white) lighter and more even in texture

— Bread is usually cooked when golden brown and slightly shrunk from sides of the loaf tin. Turn out and tap the bottom with your knuckles. If it makes a hollow sound it is cooked. If it not quite cooked, put it back in the oven, either upside down or on its side

Irish Soda Bread

This recipe has been in Jean Armstrong's family for at least 3 generations. One memory of her Irish childhood is of her grandmother making soda bread and cooking it on a hearth fire in what was known as an oven pot, with peat coals below and small pieces of glowing peat on the lid. Soft and lovely, it tasted delicious with lots of butter.

Soda bread was an important part of the family diet with 'shop bread' only bought when visitors had to be entertained. No ingredient was ever weighed – just a handful of this, a pinch of that or a spoonful of the other. The mixture was then turned out and shaped into a bannock on a big, scrubbed table, with the flour coming from a large sack in the pantry. Jean still uses hand measures, but for us she kindly worked out the specific amounts.

TIP: In smart restaurants and hotels in Ireland, an egg is often added to the mixture to give a lighter texture.

SERVES: 4-6
PREPARATION TIME: 5 minutes
COOKING TIME: 50 minutes

Pre-heat the oven to 200°C / 400°F / Gas Mark 6

340g (12oz) McDougalls granary malted brown flour
110g (4oz) plain white flour
2 teaspoons bicarbonate of soda
1 teaspoon salt
1 tablespoon dark brown muscovado sugar
50g (2oz) butter
450ml (3/4 pint) buttermilk

Put the dry ingredients into a food processor and blend until crumbly. Turn into a large bowl and rub in butter. Make a well in the centre and pour in the buttermilk. Cut in with a knife until a soft dough is formed. Turn onto a floured surface and shape gently into a round about 5cm (2") thick. Place on a greased, floured baking sheet and score a cross with a sharp knife on the surface about 2.5cm (1") deep. Bake for about 45 minutes until the base sounds hollow when knocked. Serve warm.

Caroline's Yoghurt Bread Ⓥ Ⓕ

Caroline Jeremy, who has been responsible for new recipe ideas since the company started, first made this bread as a health-conscious teenager at school in Cape Town.
Not only healthy, it takes just 10 minutes to make and doesn't even need to prove before cooking.
Eat straight from the oven whilst still slightly moist, but if there's any left the next day, Caroline's children gobble it down as toast!

MAKES 1 LOAF
PREPARATION TIME: 10 minutes COOKING TIME: 1 hour

450g (1lb) malted brown flour
1 teaspoon salt
1 level tablespoon demerara sugar
1 heaped teaspoon bicarbonate of soda
570ml (1 pint) natural whole-milk yoghurt
A dash of milk to moisten
Handful of sunflower seeds
Loaf tin approx 21x11x6cm (8½ x 4½ x 2½"), greased and floured

Pre-heat the oven to 200°C/400°F/Gas Mark 6.

Put all the dry ingredients into a bowl and mix well.

Add 425ml/¾ pint yoghurt and mix together well. It is best to use your hands. Add the rest of the yoghurt a little at a time, mixing well into the flour, until the dough is moist and quite sticky. If it is still not moist enough, add some milk.

Form the mixture into a ball, sprinkling some flour around the outside of the dough so that your hands no longer stick to it.

Press the dough into the loaf tin. Make a lengthwise indentation down the centre with a knife and sprinkle some flour or sunflower seeds into it.

Bake for 15 minutes at 200°C/400°F/Gas Mark 6. Lower the heat to 180°C/350°F/Gas Mark 4 and bake for 45 minutes. Cool on a wire rack.

Dilly Casserole Bread ⓥ ⓕ

You can make bread in any kind of ovenproof receptacle, including a tin can over an open fire. This type of yeasty, cheesy bread bakes well in a low casserole dish. Around Opelousas, Louisiana, Tony Chachere is known as the 'Ole Master' of Cajun cuisine. He appears on TV chat shows, contributes to the food pages of newspapers and runs a fishing and hunting camp on Bayou Big Alabama, where he bakes this bread. It is best served fresh and warm with most kinds of soup or gumbo, particularly fish-based recipes, as its flavours mingle pleasantly without being overly strong or dominant.

SERVES: 4
PREPARATION TIME: 1 hour 15 minutes
COOKING TIME: 40 - 50 minutes
Pre-heat the oven to 180°C / 350°F / Gas Mark 4

15g (½oz) dried yeast
65ml (2½ floz) warm water
1 egg, beaten
1 dessertspoon sugar
2 tablespoons onion, finely chopped
40g (1½oz) butter, melted
2 teaspoons dill seed
1 teaspoon salt
¼ teaspoon bicarbonate of soda
200g (7oz) cottage cheese, warmed
225g (8oz) plain flour, sifted

Grease a 20cm (8") low casserole or gratin dish.

Mix the yeast and water and leave until frothy, about 10 minutes. Combine the egg, sugar, onion, 30g (1oz) of the butter, dill seed, salt, soda and warmed cottage cheese in a bowl. Add the yeast mixture and stir well. Gradually add the sifted flour to make a stiff dough and beat well. The mixture will not be stiff enough to knead. Leave in a warm place to rise until it has doubled in size, about 1 hour, then stir briefly. Pour into the low casserole and allow to rise again for about 20-30 minutes. Bake uncovered for 40-50 minutes until brown. Cool a little and brush all over with remaining melted butter.

Seedy Bread

(V) (F)

We found this tasty bread recipe in a 1931 booklet called Cornish Recipes Ancient & Modern, published by a local group of the Women's Institute. Caraway seeds are so delicious in cheese, cakes, soups and stews that we just had to try it out. The combination of lard and caraway seeds added to a basic dough was a winner, and produces a crisp and golden crust that just melts in the mouth. This soft, springy loaf is ideal for those who mourn the decline in the use of lard!

TIP: Use the lard straight from the fridge.

SERVES: 4
PREPARATION TIME: 2 hours   COOKING TIME: 30 minutes
Pre-heat the oven to 190°C/375°F/Gas Mark 5

450g (1lb) strong white flour
1½ teaspoons salt
1 tablespoon dried yeast
4 tablespoons warm water
150ml (¼ pint) lukewarm milk
2 eggs
75g (3oz) lard, cut into small pieces
1 tablespoon caraway seeds

Grease a loaf tin measuring 25 x 10 x 7.5 cm (10 x 4 x 3").

Put the flour and salt in a large bowl. Put the yeast and water in a cup, stir and leave until frothy, about 10 minutes. Mix the milk with the eggs. Make a well in the centre of the flour and pour in the milk and egg mixture, cutting it into the flour with a knife until a dough forms, soft but not too sticky. If the dough is a little dry, add a little more milk. Turn out and knead for 5 minutes. Clean and dry the bowl, sprinkle with flour and return the dough to it. Cover with a cloth and stand in a warm place for about 1 hour, or until doubled in size.

Turn out the dough and knead in the lard and 1 teaspo of caraway seeds, until evenly distributed but not completely rubbed in. Form into a loaf and put into the greased loaf tin. Cover with a cloth and leave to rise in a warm place for 30 minutes. Sprinkle on the remaining caraway seeds and bake for 30 minutes. Cool on a wire rack.

South American Cheese Corn Bread

Corn bread is a Latin American favourite from Mexico down to Cape Horn. This wonderfully indulgent variation is both moist and springy, with an intensely cheesy Cheddar topping. Food writer Carol Wilson adapted this recipe from the basic corn bread method supplied by a South American friend and passed it on to us. It can be made more colourful by adding chopped green and red peppers.

TIP: If you don't have exactly the right size tin use a smaller one with higher sides. If the corn bread is too thin it will dry out.

SERVES: 6-8
PREPARATION TIME: 25 minutes
COOKING TIME: 45 minutes
Pre-heat the oven to 200°C /400°F/ Gas Mark 6

110g (4oz) butter
2 medium onions, finely chopped
225g (8oz) cottage cheese
225g (8oz) Cheddar cheese, grated
200g (7oz) cornmeal
250g (9oz) tinned creamed sweetcorn
1 teaspoon salt
200ml (7floz) milk
6 eggs, separated
225g (8oz) smoked bacon, cut into fine strips

Lightly grease and flour a 26 x 33cm (10 x 14") tin.

Melt half the butter and cook the onions in a covered saucepan for 5 minutes, without colouring. Set aside to cool. Put the remaining butter and onions, cottage cheese and grated Cheddar cheese into a bowl and mix well. Add the cornmeal, sweetcorn, salt and milk, stir into the cheese mixture and mix well. Whisk the egg whites to soft peaks. Beat the egg yolks and fold into the egg whites. Fold the egg mixture into the cheese mixture. Pour into a greased, floured tin, top with the strips of smoked bacon and bake for 45 minutes until cooked. Serve warm.

Cheese & Sage Damper Bread (V)

In Australia, damper is still cooked in the bush in a billy can, or in the city over barbecue coals. Traditionally, the coals of the fire are pushed to one side, the damper is placed on the ashes, and then covered over with more ashes. However, you don't have to be a pyromaniac to make a good damper - it still works well cooked on a baking sheet in the oven!

This is a really simple bread to make. Just whizz up the ingredients in the food processor, bake, and serve warm. The melted cheese and poppy seed topping make it look as irresistible as it tastes.

SERVES: 4-6
PREPARATION TIME: 10 minutes
COOKING TIME: 25-30 minutes

Pre-heat the oven to 200°C / 400°F / Gas Mark 6

110g (4oz) mature Cheddar cheese
200g (7oz) wholemeal self-raising flour
½ teaspoon paprika
¼ teaspoon freshly ground black pepper
1 teaspoon dried sage
40g (1½ oz) butter or margarine
175ml (6floz) skimmed evaporated milk
1 tablespoon milk
2 tablespoons Parmesan cheese, freshly grated
1 tablespoon poppy seeds
sea salt

Grate cheese in a food processor then add the flour, paprika, pepper, sage and butter and process until crumbly. With the motor running, gradually add the evaporated milk until a soft but not sticky dough is formed. On a lightly floured baking sheet, knead the dough very lightly into a round. Using a sharp knife, cut almost through the dough into 8 wedges.

Brush the top with milk and sprinkle with Parmesan cheese, poppy seeds and sea salt, and bake for 25-30 minutes. Cool slightly, cut into wedges and eat while fresh and warm.

Cheese & Olive Scone Bake

Mary Berry, famous for her Aga cookery courses and books, has shared one of her best bread recipes with us. In addition to teaching, Mary also makes salad dressings with her daughter Annabel, which they sell at the major agricultural shows. We usually have a fresh soup stand at these shows, and as Mary and Annabel live off our soups during exhibition days, they have become regular visitors to our stands.

This light and cake-like scone bread recipe of Mary's is quick and easy to make and goes particularly well with Mediterranean-style soups. Making one large scone is faster than rolling the dough and cutting out lots of little ones. If you don't have a roasting tin, just shape the dough into an oblong and place on a baking sheet.

SERVES: 6-8
PREPARATION TIME: 10 minutes   COOKING TIME: 35-40 minutes

Pre-heat the oven to 200°C/400°F/ Gas Mark 6

450g (1lb) plain or wholemeal self-raising flour
2 teaspoons baking powder
1 teaspoon salt
110g (4oz) butter
150g (5oz) mature Cheddar cheese, grated
110g (4oz) black Kalamata olives, pitted and finely chopped
2 eggs, broken into a measuring jug and made up to
        290ml (½ pint) with milk
25g (1oz) Parmesan cheese, freshly grated

With a brush, lightly oil a 30 x 22cm (12 x 9") roasting tin.

Put the flour, baking powder, salt and butter into a food processor and blend until the mixture resembles fine breadcrumbs. Add the Cheddar cheese and olives and, with the motor running, add the egg and milk mixture until a soft dough is formed. Alternatively, if preparing manually, put the flour, baking powder and salt into a large bowl and rub in the butter lightly with your finger tips until the mixture resembles fine breadcrumbs. Stir in the Cheddar cheese and olives. Make a well in the mixture and add the egg and milk mixture. Add 1-2 extra tablespoons of milk to bind together if necessary.

Turn out the dough onto a lightly floured surface and knead gently for about 15 seconds, until the dough is smooth. Remember, however, that this must be done quickly and gently or the resulting bread will be heavy. Roll out to an oblong shape 2.5cm (1") thick and put into a roasting tin. Mark into 12 squares and brush the top with a little milk. Sprinkle with Parmesan cheese and bake for 30-40 minutes until golden brown and well risen.

Carrot &
Parmesan Scones

The illustrator of this book, Serena Feneziani, left Rome
for London and ended up sharing a studio with our
designer Claire Fry. Serena likes cooking, especially
bread-making, and has brought many variations of
this recipe into the studio as a lunchtime treat. Her
idea for these heavenly scones came from a feature
on cooking with potatoes in an Italian newspaper.
She experimented with the original recipe for potato
& Parmesan scones, adding bacon and tweaking the
other ingredients. This is a nice easy recipe to make
and well worth the effort, comforting and moreish
- don't expect to be able to save any for the freezer.
We've tried it substituting sweet potato for the
potato - delicious!

SERVES: 4
PREPARATION AND COOKING TIME: 30 minutes
Pre-heat oven to 180°C/350°F/Gas Mark 4

110g (4oz) smoked bacon rashers
225g (8oz) potato, peeled and chopped
225g (8oz) carrot, peeled and grated
225ml (8 floz) milk
250g (9oz) unbleached organic white flour
1 sachet Easy Bake yeast
75g (3oz) Parmesan cheese, grated
1 egg
1 tablespoon extra virgin olive oil
pinch salt

Grill the bacon until crisp. Cut up into small pieces.
Place the potato, carrot and milk in a liquidiser and
process until smooth.

Combine all of the remaining ingredients in a
separate bowl and beat together well. Add the bacon
and milk mixture, and stir together to make a wet
dough. Spoon the dough onto a greased baking sheet
in drop scones of 4cm (2") in diameter. Bake in the
oven for 20 minutes until golden brown. Serve straight
from the oven. They can also be re-heated.

Buckwheat Blinis

(V)

These small, yeasty Russian pancakes, cooked in a skillet, frying pan or a griddle, are traditionally served with a topping of sour cream and caviar. The nutty texture of the buckwheat, a standard Russian staple, gives a superb taste and texture to these pancakes. We think they are perfect with soup, either on their own, or spread with butter. Alternatively eat them the traditional Russian way, topped with smoked salmon, sour cream, a squeeze of lemon juice and black pepper. Serve warm.

SERVES: 8
PREPARATION AND COOKING TIME: 2 hours 25 minutes
(inc. 1½ hours to set in a warm place)

1 packet active dry yeast
175ml (6floz) warm water
300ml (11 floz) milk
250g (9oz) plain flour
125g (4½ oz) buckwheat flour
3 eggs, separated
½ teaspoon salt
pinch of sugar
175g (6oz) melted unsalted butter
(plus additional butter for cooking)

Combine the yeast and warm water in a bowl, cover with a cloth and set aside in a warm place to prove for 15 minutes.

Put the yeast mixture, milk, flours, egg yolks, salt, sugar and melted butter in a blender or food processor. Blend at high speed for 40 seconds. Turn the machine off, scrape down the sides of the container, then blend for another few seconds. (If you are mixing the ingredients by hand, beat together in a bowl with a whisk). Pour the batter into a bowl that is large enough to accommodate the rising. Cover loosely and set in a warm place to rise for 1½ to 2 hours. Do not let the batter rise much longer or the blini will taste overfermented. Heat a heavy skillet, griddle or blini pan. Brush with melted butter. Drop batter by the tablespoon onto the hot pan. Turn the blini when the first side is lightly browned and cook briefly on the other side. Keep the blinis on a heated platter until all the batter is used up.

Corn & Chilli Muffins

These warm muffins taste sensational and are hard to resist served with a creamy or spicy soup. Try with Spicy Corn Chowder (see page 73).

MAKES 12 MUFFINS
PREPARATION AND COOKING TIME: 35 minutes
Preheat oven to 200°C/400°F/Gas Mark 6

110g (4oz) plain flour
110g (4oz) yellow cornmeal
2 teaspoons baking powder
½ teaspoon bicarbonate of soda
½ teaspoon salt
175ml (6oz) sour cream
2 medium-sized eggs
50g (2oz) unsalted butter, melted
25g (1oz) green Jalapeño chillies, deseeded and finely chopped
25g (1oz) red Jalapeño chillies, deseeded and finely chopped
50g (2oz) mature Cheddar, finely grated

1 cake or muffin tin

Sift together the flour, cornmeal, baking powder, bicarbonate of soda and salt, then set aside. In a separate bowl whisk together the sour cream, eggs and melted butter until smooth and just combined. Then stir in the chillies and cheese. Add to the flour mixture and stir to blend completely. Spoon into greased cake or muffin tins, filling each approximately two-thirds full. Bake for 15 minutes or until a toothpick inserted in the centre of the muffin comes out clean. Cool a little before serving.

Zwiebel Kuchen

One of prize-winning food writer, novelist and natural history artist Elisabeth Luard's best-known books is The Rich Tradition of European Peasant Cookery, an inspiring book featuring recipes from all over Europe. This German onion bread was a recipe we originally pulled out of the Sunday Telegraph Magazine. It's rather like a very luxurious onion pizza and looks marvellous.

SERVES: 4
PREPARATION AND COOKING TIME: 1 hour 15 minutes
Pre-heat the oven to 220°C / 425°F / Gas Mark 7

FOR THE BASE:
400g (14oz) strong white bread flour, plus a little extra for dusting
50g (2oz) fresh yeast, or 25g (1oz) dried yeast and a pinch of sugar,
        mixed with 1 tablespoon of the milk to liquidise
1 teaspoon dried marjoram
110g (4oz) butter or lard
2 level teaspoons salt
150ml (¼ pint) milk
150ml (¼ pint) water

FOR THE TOPPING:
25g (1oz) butter
2 tablespoons extra virgin olive oil
6-8 red onions, finely sliced, into rings
110g (4oz) smoked streaky bacon, finely chopped
a little oil to grease the tin
2 eggs
100ml (4 floz) soured cream
½ teaspoon grated nutmeg
salt and freshly ground black pepper

If making the dough by hand, put the flour, yeast, marjoram and salt into a bowl and, using the tips of your fingers, work the butter or lard into the flour until the mixture resembles fine crumbs. Make a well in the centre and pour in the milk and water. Cut the liquid into the flour with a knife and, when beginning to form a dough, use your hand to bring the dough together. Dust a work surface with flour and tip out the dough. Knead for 1 minute until a smooth dough is formed and place in a floured bowl. Cover and leave in a warm place to rise for 30 minutes. Alternatively, put all the base ingredients into a food processor and blend until a wet dough is formed. Turn out onto a floured surface and continue as before.

For the topping, heat the butter and oil and fry the finely sliced onions and bacon gently for about 30 minutes until soft and caramelised.

Brush a baking sheet with oil and tip the dough onto it. Sprinkle with a little flour and press out to the thickness of your hand. Top with the onions and bacon, leaving 2.5cm (1") uncovered around the edge. Mix the eggs, soured cream and nutmeg, taste for seasoning, then trickle over the onions, starting in the middle so it doesn't flow over the edge. Bake for 20-25 minutes or until the dough is well risen and browned. Delicious hot, warm or at room temperature.

Spiced Herb Bread   Ⓥ Ⓕ

Garlic bread seems slightly passé once you have tried this easy fresh herb and spice variation. Ideal for having with soup at picnics and barbecues, the bread can be kept warm by keeping it in the foil and wrapping in lots of newspaper.

Fenugreek is an aromatic Mediterranean plant originating in the Middle East. It produces long slender curved pods containing flat brownish seeds, which are then roasted and ground. Today, fenugreek is usually added to curries, but in North Africa, the seeds used to be ground into flour, then mixed with olive oil and caster sugar to fatten women.

SERVES : 4
PREPARATION TIME: 15 minutes
COOKING TIME: 15 minutes

Pre-heat the oven to 200°C / 400°F / Gas Mark 6

1 ciabatta, baguette or granary stick
75g (3oz) butter
1 garlic clove, crushed
1 dessertspoon tomato purée
1 dessertspoon fresh coriander leaves, chopped
1 tablespoon fresh flat leaf parsley, chopped
½ teaspoon ground cumin
pinch of ground cloves
pinch of ground fenugreek
salt and freshly ground black pepper

Slice the loaf almost through to the base in 2.5cm (1") diagonal slices. Cream the remaining ingredients together and spread between each slice. Spread any remaining butter all over the bread. Seal in foil and bake for 10 minutes. Open the foil and bake for a further 5 minutes. Serve hot.

Other things

Other things

In our final chapter we have looked at all the different things we plonk onto a soup. Any little extras that can be dolloped, sprinkled, arranged, drizzled or floated on a bowl to add a whole new dimension and perhaps a touch of panache.

It is these little things that can completely transform a soup by bringing not only colour and flavour, but also texture and substance. Whilst an undressed bowl of soup allows you to really enjoy the flavours, by always ignoring the vast array of things that can be added, you may be missing out on the full potential of the recipe.

All these toppings can add precisely what your mood dictates. It may be stodge, it may be refinement, it may be texture, it may be colour. The alternatives are endless.

We have listed some of our favourites, but the most important thing is to experiment. What might be right for one day will not necessarily be right for the next. Just use your common sense. Almost anything goes as long as it reflects, or contrasts with, the flavour of the soup. The only boundary is your imagination.

Have fun and experiment!

Simple Garnishes

An A-Z Guide

ALMONDS – toasted almonds are perfect plonked on top of Leek & Carrot Soup.

AVOCADO PEAR – slices of ripe avocado pear are delicious on Vichyssoise or spicy beans. Slice at the last moment so they don't go brown.

BACON – try pieces of crispy bacon on top of Vichyssoise or Spinach & Nutmeg Soup. Also use to garnish Fresh Baked Beans (see page 77).

BASIL – as with all large-leaved herbs, basil bruises easily, so slice thin slithers by placing one leaf on top of another, roll them up from the base of the stem and, with a sharp knife, thinly slice cross the rolled leaves. Excellent for garnishing Mediterranean-style dishes.

CALVADOS – add a dash together with a sprinkling of cinnamon to vegetable soups.

CARROT – carrot 'tagliatelle' (thinly sliced into ribbons and simmered until tender) goes well with root vegetable soups.

CHEESE – you can't go wrong with grated cheese. Try grating Gruyère onto slices of dry or lightly toasted baguette, float the slices on top of bowls of hot soup and then grill them until the cheese turns golden brown. Or try shavings of fresh Parmesan or Pecorino cheese in Tomato & Basil Vichyssoise (see page 37) or crumbled feta cheese in tomato soup. Add mature grated Cheddar to Fresh Baked Beans (see page 77).

CHERRY TOMATOES – float halved cherry tomatoes and basil leaves in chilled summer soups, especially Tomato & Basil Vichyssoise (see page 37).

CHILLIES – finely sliced green chillies add bite to Thai Spinach Soup (see page 57).

CHIVES – fresh snipped chives are good on almost any kind of soup, but go particularly well with the classic Vichyssoise. Don't forget chive flowers look fabulous floating with snipped chives and a swirl of cream on chilled soups such as Potato, Leek & Lavender Soup (see page 17).

COCONUT – toasted parings of coconut with lime and lemon zest are good with an Asian-style soup. Try with Thai Spinach Soup (see page 57).

COGNAC – Lovely in French Onion Soup.

CREAM – a swirl of single or double cream adds creaminess to all sorts of soups, especially summer recipes; or try stirring in chopped herbs to thick (but not stiff) cream with some salt and pepper and float spoonfuls on top of winter soups; soured cream and chopped spring onions are delicious in Asparagus Soup. We often use crème fraîche as an alternative for its lightness and delicate flavour. Chilli con carne needs sour cream for coolness and contrast and other strongly spiced bean dishes benefit from a substantial dollop.

CUCUMBER RAITA – made with diced cucumber and natural yoghurt. This goes wonderfully with Indian soups like Bengal Lancer's (see page 53).

FILO PASTRY SHAPES – try moon and star shapes filled with a mixture of cheese and chopped nuts.

FLOWERS – flowers have been used in cooking for centuries. Add edible blossoms to decorate summer soups or try floating with chopped herbs or slices of fruit. The centres of nasturtium blossoms can be stuffed with crème fraîche or goats' cheese.

ICE CREAM – if you make your own ice-cream, think about adding a big spoonful to a chilled sweet soup.

Dumplings & Gnocchi

Bread is not the only way to add comforting 'stodge' to a dish. Dumplings and gnocchi can be deceptively simple to make. They contribute different flavours as well as substance. Here are some ideas:

CHEESE & SPINACH DUMPLINGS

SERVES: 6
PREPARATION AND COOKING TIME: 30 minutes

25g (1oz) butter
450g (1lb) spinach leaves, washed, dried thoroughly and chopped
450g (1lb) Ricotta cheese
1 tablespoon parsley, finely chopped
1 garlic clove, finely chopped
225g (8oz) self-raising flour
½ teaspoon salt and freshly ground black pepper
2 eggs

Melt the butter in a large saucepan, add the spinach and cook for 2-3 minutes over a medium heat. Remove from the heat and leave to cool. Combine the cheese, spinach, parsley, garlic, ½ the flour, salt and pepper together in a bowl. Add the eggs, 1 by 1, and work into the flour mixture, then slowly add the remaining flour until you have a firm but malleable dough. Roll into 12-15 small balls. Cook in boiling, salted water for 15-20 minutes.
Light and delicious with Pumpkin or Tomato Soup.

HERBY PANCETTA DUMPLINGS

This is cookery writer Pippin Britz's recipe. She recommends it with Celeriac & Mushroom Soup (see our Celeriac & Porcini Soup on page 38). Also delicious with Pea or Tomato Soup or Chicken, Lemon & Tarragon Soup.

SERVES: 6
PREPARATION AND COOKING TIME: 25 minutes

100g (4oz) self-raising flour
35g (1½oz) fresh white breadcrumbs
50g (2oz) vegetable suet
110g (4oz) pancetta, finely diced
1 teaspoon fresh tarragon, chopped
1 tablespoon celery leaves, chopped
salt and freshly ground black pepper
water to bind

Combine all the ingredients in a bowl, except the water. Mix well to evenly distribute the ingredients, then slowly add about 3 tablespoons of water to form a soft dough. Roll into small balls approximately 2cm (1") in diameter and drop into your choice of soup. Simmer for about 10 minutes until fluffed and cooked through.

LITTLE STAR ANISE DUMPLINGS

A finalist from one of our soup competitions, Susan Riddy, gave us this unusual dumpling recipe to go with her Far East Hot Turkey Soup (see page 58). Star Anise, which gives these dumplings their slightly sweet aniseed taste, can be found in good supermarkets or Chinese grocers.

SERVES: 6
PREPARATION AND COOKING TIME: 20 minutes

4 whole star anise, husks discarded, ground in pestle and mortar, or use ready-ground star anise

Puff Pastry Tops

This deliciously flaky topping can form a lid for any winter soup- i
as well as making it a little more substantial. Vegetarian cook an
Scott Morgan often gives us suggestions. This is her recipe.

SERVES: 4

Pre-heat the oven to 220°C/425°F/Gas Mark 7

250g (9oz) puff pastry

1 egg, beaten

Ladle chilled soup into 4 ovenproof bowls. Roll out the pastry very thi
surface. Cut into 4 circles a little larger than the rim of the bowls, allowing a
Brush the edge of the circles with beaten egg. Place a pastry circle over
gently but firmly, using the egg to attach the pastry to the bowl. Trim the
surface with the remaining egg. Chill well. Place the soup bowls on a baki
20 minutes until well risen and golden brown and the soup is piping ho

Salsas & Relishes

When we asked Paul Bloomfield, one of our recipe testers, if he
recipe, we didn't anticipate quite such a good response. He once
Dallas, Texas and all these salsas regularly appeared on his menu.
our various bean cakes and some of our American-style bean dish
& Mango Relish is an exception, as it is rather too full of beans itse
another bean dish, but it's so good that we couldn't resist includin

CARIBBEAN SALSA

SERVES: 4

PREPARATION TIME: 25 minutes

2 tablespoons red onion, finely diced
150g (5oz) tomato, peeled,
de-seeded and finely chopped
1 jalapeño chilli, de-seeded and finely diced
4 tablespoons basil leaves, freshly chopped

1 red pepper, de-se
5mm (¼
juice of 2
60g (2½oz) fresh p
5mm (¼
¼ teaspo

Combine all the ingredients in a bowl and refrigerate for at least 30 m
excellent with grilled fish, lobster or chicken.

BLACK BEAN RELISH & MANGO

SERVES: 4

PREPARATION AND COOKING TIME: overnight soaking of beans plus 1 1

150g (5oz) black beans, soaked overnight and
cooked for 1½ hours then cooled
150g (5oz) mango, peeled and diced
2 teaspoons white wine vinegar

2 teaspoons m
2 tablespoons fresh coria
salt and freshly gro
squeeze of le

Combine the beans, mango, vinegar, maple syrup and coriander in a bowl
for 5 minutes. Adjust the flavour with salt, pepper and lemon juice and refri

---

1 teaspoon freshly grated nutmeg
1 teaspoon salt
50g (2oz) vegetarian suet
110g (4oz) self-raising flour
water to bind
850ml (1½ pints) vegetable or meat stock with star anise husks added

Combine all the ingredients together in a bowl, except the water. Mix well and slowly add
sufficient water to hold the dumplings together. Do not make the dumpling mixture too sticky-
add more flour if necessary. Roll the dumpling mixture into small balls approximately 2cm (1")
in diameter. Bring stock to the boil and drop the dumplings in. Lower heat to prevent them
breaking up. Cook for 10-12 minutes until they float to the surface. Remove with a slotted spoon
and add to individual bowls.

TIP: don't be tempted to cook these dumplings in the soup: they can absorb too much of the
liquid and cloud it.

CHILLI GNOCCHI

Alastair Little and Richard Whittington created this delicious gnocchi recipe.

SERVES: 4

PREPARATION AND COOKING TIME: 50 minutes

675g (1½lb) potatoes, peeled and cut into large chunks
4 fresh red chillies or to taste, seeded and finely shredded
handful of fresh coriander leaves, roughly chopped
salt and freshly ground black pepper
finely grated nutmeg to taste
200g (7oz) self-raising flour, plus a little more for dusting
1 medium egg

Put the potatoes into a saucepan, cover with cold salted water, bring to the boil and simmer
gently for about 20 minutes until tender. Drain, return to the pan and shake over a low heat to
evaporate excess moisture. Add the chillies and chopped coriander leaves, season with salt,
pepper and grated nutmeg. Mash well until free of lumps. Transfer to a bowl, add the flour and
beat briefly to amalgamate. Beat in the egg, then turn out onto a floured surface.

Knead the mixture briefly so as not to overwork, then divide into 4. Roll each piece with your
hands into a 2.5cm (1") cylinder. Cut into 2.5cm (1") dumplings. Drop the dumplings into boiling
salted water. When they rise to the surface, they are cooked and ready to garnish your soup.

PUMPKIN & ROCKET GNOCCHI

SERVES: 4

PREPARATION AND COOKING TIME: 60 minutes

675g (1½lb) pumpkin, peeled and cut into 2.5cm (1") pieces
110g (4oz) plain flour, sifted
50g (2oz) parmesan cheese, freshly grated
50g (2oz) fresh rocket leaves, roughly chopped
50g (2oz) fresh basil leaves, roughly chopped
salt and freshly ground black pepper
1 egg

Put the pumpkin into a saucepan, cover with salted water, bring to the boil and simmer gently
for 5-10 minutes until tender. Drain well, then mash until smooth. Add the sifted flour and beat
briefly to amalgamate. Add the Parmesan, rocket and basil, and taste for seasoning. Beat in the
egg, then turn out onto a floured surface.

Knead the mixture briefly so as not to overwork, then divide into 4. Roll each piece with your
hands into a 2.5cm (1") cylinder. Cut into 2.5cm (1") dumplings. Drop the dumplings into boiling
salted water. When they rise to the surface, they are cooked and ready to garnish your soup.

Potato Recipes

FLAVOURED MASH

If mashed potato to you means little more than just a bland
these. Match them up with a bean dish or your favourite cas
tablespoon or two of mash to a bowl of soup, turning it into

Add any of these mixtures to cooked potatoes. Stir in l
needed, add more moisture with butter, hot milk or oli

Pesto
Tapenade
Roasted garlic & chilli: roast garlic for 20 minutes in oven. Skin, c
finely chopped red chilli and olive oil
Grated cheese
Mixed with puréed celeriac
Grainy mustard
Capers mixed with yoghurt
Fenugreek, toasted coriander seeds and y
Sour cream, puréed avocado and finely choppe
Toasted pine nuts and goats' cheese
Zest and juice of a lime with coconut and co
Soy sauce, honey and Chinese five spi
Try mashing cooked swede with potatoes, butter and seasoniu
Mash boiled sweet potatoes with butter and fr
Serve plain mashed potato topped with some of our flavoured

SPICY BERMUDIAN BARBECUE PO

We tried hard to match these with something in the book and faile
decided to include it anyway. Clare Anderton learnt this deliciou
was working hard in Bermuda for several years, in between saili
tennis balls and attending barbecues.

SERVES: 1
PREPARATION TIME: 5 minutes COOKING TIME:
Pre-heat the barbecue or the oven to 200°C/450°F.

250g (9oz) potatoes, peeled and cut into 2.5cm
¼ medium onion, finely chopped
extra virgin olive oil to coat everything
¼ teaspoon paprika
½ teaspoon Cajun seasoning, to taste
1 tablespoon fresh herbs, chopped e.g. mint, parsley and

Mix everything together, then pile onto a large square of foil. Fol
parcel and place on a barbecue or in the oven for about 45 w
tender, serve piping hot from the foil.

SPRING ONION CREAM SALSA

SERVES: 4
PREPARATION TIME: 30 minutes
100ml (4floz) sour cream
2 tablespoons rice wine vinegar
2 tablespoons mushroom soy sauce
1 teaspoon grated ginger
2 shallots, peeled and finely chopped
1 garlic clove, peeled and finely chopped
1 serrano chilli, de-seeded and finely chopped
4 spring onions, white part only, finely chopped
1 tablespoon fresh mint leaves, chopped
1 tablespoon fresh coriander leaves, chopped
salt and freshly ground black pepper
lime juice, to taste

Combine the sour cream, vinegar, soy sauce, ginger, shallots, garlic, chilli and spring onions
together in a bowl. Leave for 10 minutes to infuse. Add fresh herbs and lime juice, then season
to taste. Refrigerate until ready to use.

SWEETCORN & APPLE RELISH

SERVES: 4
PREPARATION TIME: 30 minutes
1 medium red apple, diced, peel on
1 medium Granny Smith apple, diced, peel on
275g (10oz) sweetcorn, cooked
5 spring onions, white part only, finely chopped
½ red pepper, finely diced
½ green pepper, finely diced
1 tablespoon rice wine vinegar
½ tablespoon white wine vinegar
salt and freshly ground black pepper
lemon juice, to taste

Combine the apples, sweetcorn, spring onions, peppers and vinegars in a bowl, and leave for
5 minutes to infuse. Season and add lemon juice to taste. Refrigerate until ready to use.

MANGO PICO-DE-GALLO

SERVES: 4
PREPARATION TIME: 15 minutes
2 ripe mangoes, peeled and cut into 5mm (¼") dice
1 tomato, peeled, de-seeded and cut into 5mm (¼") dice
½ red onion, peeled and cut into 5mm (¼") dice
1 garlic clove, finely chopped
2 jalapeño chillies, de-seeded and finely chopped
1 tablespoon fresh coriander leaves, finely chopped
pinch chilli powder
3 tablespoons lime juice
salt and freshly ground black pepper

Combine the mangoes, tomato, red onion, garlic, chillies, coriander and chilli powder. Mix well,
stir in the lime juice, taste for seasoning.

Sambals

Traditionally eaten with Oriental dishes, sambals are generally designed to bring out the spiciness in the main dish - although many are spicy enough in their own right! Here we've included a recipe for a hot sambal as well as a milder, raita-style relish, both are delicious with soups or beans.

TOMATO, CORIANDER & CHILLI SAMBAL

SERVES: 4
PREPARATION TIME: 25 minutes
3 medium tomatoes, peeled, de-seeded and chopped
1 medium onion, finely chopped
2 tablespoons fresh coriander leaves, chopped
1 red chilli, de-seeded and finely chopped
salt and freshly ground black pepper

Combine tomatoes, onion, coriander leaves and chilli in a bowl. Taste for seasoning and chill until required.

CUCUMBER SAMBAL

SERVES: 4
PREPARATION TIME: 10 minutes
150g (5oz) cucumber, peeled, de-seeded and chopped
50g (2oz) unsweetened desiccated coconut
100 ml (4fl oz) natural yoghurt
2 tablespoons flaked almonds
1 tablespoon mint leaves, freshly chopped
½ teaspoon salt
pinch freshly ground black pepper

Mix all the ingredients together and chill until ready to use.

Soup Lollies

Elizabeth Wilkinson, who works in our sales department, gave us this great idea. It makes a nutritious treat for children of all ages and is terribly simple to make. Just liquidise any vegetables or fruit until they can be easily poured. Then pour into the open end of a new rubber glove so that it fills all the fingers and most of the hand, putting a wooden lolly stick in the base before securing it with string or an elastic band. Place in the freezer for 4 to 5 hours (the length of time will depend on the size of the glove) or until it is frozen solid. When you want to eat it, peel off the glove and you'll have a marvellous hand-shaped, healthy treat. You could experiment with shapes too, twisting or tying the glove into an animal shape or a victory sign before freezing it.

Grown-up versions are a novel way of cooling down on a hot day - imagine sucking on a frozen lolly of semi-puréed chewy tomato soup and coming across bits of baby tomato. Vegetable soups with a low fat content are best for this: just pour the soup into lolly moulds, insert the lolly sticks and freeze for at least 4 hours or until solid.

(V) = Suitable for Vegetarians   (F) = Suitable for Home Freezing